There's Only One Way to Win

Lessons from a Legend

Modern Success Principles from an Old-School Coach

Dick DeVenzio

Foreword by Billy Packer

www.pgcbasketball.com

Third Edition

PGC BASKETBALL

There's Only One Way to Win: Lessons from a Legend
Published by PGC Basketball

For more information about our books, visit our website at www.pgcbasketball.com, or email us at info@pgcbasketball.com.

Library of Congress Control Number: 2006925010

ISBN: 978-0-9839380-5-7

Original Publication Date: January 15, 1993

For information, purchases or permissions, go to:
http://www.pgcbasketball.com

To my mother
Who would have been thrilled
To share this book with my father

"[Chuck] DeVenzio is colorful. The antics he goes through during a game are almost as much fun to watch as the game itself. One time I remember sitting in the dressing room at halftime of a game we were losing when DeVenzio came in and fired an orange across the room. Later, not a piece of the orange could be found. We went on to win...

"He is as good a coach as there is. He can scream, chew out and praise with the best of them. He can make players angry enough to get every drop of effort from them. He can whip a team up to a fever pitch."

— Ron Brogan
Sportswriter
Former player of Coach DV

Table of Contents

1. "He Must Be Crazy!" Page 3
Sort of a pre-game warm-up . . . all about Coach DV: his success, his colorful, idiosyncratic style that turned off so many unknowing fans, but turned on so many athletes.

Part I: Laying the Groundwork

2. The Basics Page 11
Coach DV's things that 'go without saying.' Practice on your own, play like a human being, always be ready, never give an easy basket.

3. Play like a Human Being! Page 17
It's not as easy as it sounds . . . never trot, always get a hand up, never stand straight up . . . just play with common sense.

4. Mooooove! Page 22
The one great commandment.

5. Coach DV's Four Rules of Basketball Page 28
Throw it to your own team, always move (fast), only take easy shots and don't give them any.

Part II: Irrefutable Logic, Colorful Style

6. Crap, Impatience, Vision, Parents, Pianos, Fairness, and Life Itself Page 35
A broader view of things.

7. Bluntness, Sensitivity—Tungo, Tungo, Tungo —A Hand is a Thing! Page 41
Making it all abundantly clear.

8. Blaming the Best Page 47
Who else?

9. A Commitment to Unfairness and the Importance of *Reducing* Confidence Page 52
DV was more afraid of their shots than they were afraid of shooting!

10. Focus and Learning from Victories Page 58
Bigsy's best game is marred.

11. Principles and Excuses Page 67
Epic clash.

12. "We're Ahead!" Page 72
Turns out he said exactly what he meant.

13. Errors Beget Errors Page 77
And they tend to magnify, too.

14. "Don't Get Fouled!" Page 82
Yes, you CAN help it.

15. Appearances Count Page 86
But the clothes don't make the man.

16. Injuries and the One-Second Decision Page 91
"Get up! You're not hurt!"

17. Building Confidence: Offhanded Comments, SCORE! and the Good Lord Page 96
Working in strange ways.

18. The Perfectionist Philosophy: Insurmountable Leads, Early Celebrations, and the Halftime Talk Page 105
If only they hadn't given those two baskets.

19. Etiquette and Every-time Reinforcement Page 113
How to win friends and influence people - and pour it on.

20. Wasted Timeouts, Grabby-Grabby, Page 121
and *You can beat anybody!*
He actually called it after one second, but the refs had slow reflexes.

21. Purity: Correcting the Other Team Page 133
and War on the Beaches
He just couldn't stand it any longer.

22. Auxiliary Players: Changing with the Times Page 143
Nah, the game ain't passed him by.

23. Films, newspapers, and champions Page 152
The kid would've gotten an 'A' in Current Events.

24. The Exhilaration of Approval Page 159
Nice work if you can get it.

Appendix: People Talk About Coach DV Page 171
Index Page 181

Foreword
By Billy Packer

Anyone who has played the game, had an opportunity to coach the game, or who some time in the future hopes to do either will find *There's Only One Way to Win* a fascinating and enjoyable book.

My father was a coach and, therefore, I can fully appreciate the extent to which Dick DeVenzio recaptures his experiences and insights into his dad's lifelong work as a teacher and coach of young men.

The fact that Coach Chuck DeVenzio is one of the all time most successful high school coaches in America is relatively unimportant in regard to the message delivered in this book. This is not a book of the exact science of basketball X's and O's, but rather an insight into the methods and philosophy of how the game of basketball and life should be played, through the thoughts and beliefs of one who gained great success and internal satisfaction—the satisfaction of establishing goals, values, and work ethic.

"The friendships you forge on a championship team are likely to stay with you for the rest of your life. You can feel it and never forget it; it will last forever." Coach DeVenzio discusses the championship attitude and spirit and defines the true championship feeling that one can impart only after many years of experience.

"We don't want our poor shooters to feel confident; we don't want our poor shooters shooting. People claim you need balanced scoring, but you don't. You need all of your players to do just what they are good at." You have just read a deep statement, one which contradicts many of the philosophies of some great coaches, but it is just the type of philosophy which sets Coach DeVenzio apart from the norm.

"The final score of any game should reflect the actual difference in the skills and performance level of the two teams; otherwise, the whole meaning of sports and competition is prostituted." Once again, Coach DeVenzio's philosophy gives insight into many aspects of working with young people. Why do you substitute, why do you push to excel, what is really important about playing the game?

I can assure you that, at whatever level you are presently coaching or participating, this book will give you a greater understanding of the game and how one man who has been very successful sees it. You may not agree with every point, but you will be required to think and therefore it's a certainty that you will enjoy *There's Only One Way to Win*.

— Billy Packer
June 1992

1.
HE MUST BE CRAZY!
An Introduction to Coach DV

Chuck DeVenzio's style of coaching high school basketball doesn't endear him to a lot of parents. Like a Marine Corps drill instructor, he screams incessantly at his players in a voice raspy and coarse from thirty years of abuse. When they mess up on the court, he calls them names—not always nice names. And during timeouts, well, good luck if you're the kid who just blew the slam dunk. But DeVenzio wins . . .

— Dale Gowing
Sportswriter

HE JUST GOT A GROUP OF KIDS AND TRIED TO SHOW THEM HOW TO PLAY THE GAME . . .

"He Must Be Crazy!"

People who aren't real winners—most of us—seem to have trouble understanding those few people who are.

Most people who observed Coach Chuck DeVenzio coaching a high school basketball game were usually amazed at the energy he put out or confused and irritated by his yelling and screaming. Some were truly amused and enthralled by his antics. But everyone, some begrudgingly, could not help but admire his results.

At a tiny high school in Western Pennsylvania, at a larger school in a declining steel town that hadn't had a winning team in twenty years, at one of Pennsylvania's largest, most affluent high schools, at a small private school in North Carolina, back at two tiny schools where he got his start—with rich kids and poor kids, with all White players or nearly all Blacks, with big guys who went on to college and the pros, and with little guys who went nowhere—Coach DeVenzio (Coach DV, or DV, to all who knew him) won championships. At two schools, he won where they had never won before. He was a one-man change of attitude and tradition. In a coaching career that actually began while still in college, he won over 1,000 games.

In a nutshell, Coach DV knew how to win.

His preseason talks to the players at new schools when he took over were the same as his talks to players at schools where he'd been for years:

"Boys, I've been in sports a long time. I love sports and I love to win. And I've been lucky, boys. I've been associated with winning teams my whole life; I'm too old to change that now."

He meant that he simply would not accept losing.

"We have the ingredients necessary to win this year, boys; so I expect us to win . . . We may drop a game here or there, but not many. There's no reason that you guys need to lose many games.

We just have to work hard, do what's right, and we'll be fine.

"You see, for some reason, and I've never been able to figure out why, most teams love to crap around and waste time or play like wild men or horses' tails." (The mere thought of players playing sports like wild men or like horses' tails would bring back painful memories and examples to him, his face would contort and get red, his voice would rise and get even gruffer than normal, and he'd be angry.) "Boys, there's *no reason* to play like horses' tails. There's no reason to play like a bunch of wild men. You just do what's right. It's very simple. You just play like human beings.

"That's what we're going to do this year. We're going to work hard and we're gonna *play basketball,* and we should beat just about all of the teams we play."

For Coach DV, the term "play *bas*ketball" (heavy accent on that first syllable) had special meaning. It wasn't something he threw out casually, and it meant nothing like participating or engaging in contests by running up and down on a basketball court. It meant playing the game "the way it's supposed to be played"—the *only* way, the *one way,* Coach DV's way.

"We'll have some games where the other team doesn't play like horses' tails, and then we'll have to work hard and hope some of our shots fall and some of theirs don't.

"But boys, make up your mind right now, if you want to play on this team, make up your mind you're going *to play*. Because I'm not here to crap around. I'm here to win, boys. That's what it's all about. That's what we're going to do. Make up your minds right now.

"Everyone . . . take a couple of laps."

The greatest pep talk in the world? The stuff IBM and General Motors will be clamoring to give out at their next big conventions? Hardly.

The words don't seem to say all that much. What are horses' tails? What does he mean, play like human beings? Just what is "playing *bas*ketball"? What does he mean about crapping around? How do you break down his "one way" to win?

Surely a coach with forty consecutive years of winning seasons would have dozens of secret techniques. Surely, right?

Wrong.

He didn't win for forty years by teaching fancy footwork or by coming up with ideas or plays that no one else knew about.

When asked to speak at a coaches' clinic, his first inclination was to say no. He didn't really have anything to say.

"You could just talk about your philosophy," the clinic director might suggest.

And he would answer, in all sincerity, "I don't have a philosophy. We just go out there and work hard and try to play *bas*ketball."

It didn't seem like a philosophy to him. He couldn't articulate a group of principles. He didn't like clinics himself. Didn't go to many. He considered them a waste of time.

"Coaches go there and sit around and bull," he would say, "and they all claim they do this and that, and I never see all that when we play them. Their guys crap around and play like horses' tails."

Usually, he would catch himself. "No, I shouldn't say that. I remember [so-and-so] had a good team that one year. They played some pretty good basketball. Clinics are probably great. I'm just saying that I personally never got much out of them that I could use, but they're probably great for a young coach starting out. Yeah, I think they're good."

The reason I, Coach DV's son, wrote this book and not Coach DV himself is that he didn't think much about articulating his ideas or philosophy. He believed that he never really did anything. Year after year, he just got a group of kids and tried to show them how to play the game like basketball players, like human beings.

Later in his career, when clinic directors or sportswriters would call him and ask him to speak or ask for an interview about his philosophies, he would often suggest that they get in touch with me. "My son knows my philosophies better than I do," he would explain. "How about calling him? Would you mind? I think he would be glad to talk to you." Then he would hasten to add, "I hope you don't think I'm trying to put you off. I would be happy to talk with you. I think, though, that my son will be able to give you a better idea of what you want, and then if you have any further questions, feel free to call back and I'll be happy to talk with you as long as you like."

He wanted to make sure they got something. By the time his legendary career was ending, I had finally convinced him that he did have a philosophy. At times I even rehearsed it with him—all of the lessons that I had learned personally and observed over the years—and he would say, "Yeah, that's what we tried to do! But how 'bout you talking to the guy—if you don't mind."

So I would talk to the guy, to the reporter or the young coach, and recite with a sense of awe the value of the many lessons I and so many other players had learned throughout the years.

Years later, many players would point to the experience of playing for Coach DV as the single most intense experience of their lives.

He had some innate characteristics, intolerance, and instincts that created and maintained the intensity. First, Coach DV had a tremendous eye for talent. He would always claim, modestly and sincerely, that he didn't. "I'm just not a good judge of talent," he would say, but within thirty seconds of looking at a basketball court, even when distracted by a conversation, he would know who the best players were! If you asked, he'd say he wasn't sure who had ability and he would need time to "really watch." But if you pressed him, he would say, "Well, so far, I like that kid; and that kid in the blue shirt looks like he may be able to play a little." Invariably, those two turned out to be the best players on the court.

Coach DV's judgment on players was infallible. If you asked Coach DV at a camp, for example, to give a kid some pointers, he could watch the kid for five minutes and give him more usable and helpful instructions than a whole staff of coaches watching for hours. He had a gift for stripping everything to the bone, for seeing the essence of things immediately and clearly.

When coaching his own teams, Coach DV had a rare quality which gave each player the impression that he was being watched more closely than anyone else. "Coach picks on me. Sure, he yells at everyone, but he watches me especially closely. He never misses anything I do wrong."

He never missed anything anyone did wrong.

If there is a cornerstone to his philosophy—or more appropriately, to his personality and modus operandi—it is this: vigorously, adamantly, and angrily identify every mistake, every time. Never (this cannot be over-emphasized) *never* let a mistake pass. *Never* let anything but total effort pass for adequate. From the bat boy or ball boy to the star player, *never* let a bad thing go uncorrected. Everyone is the same when it comes to errors. If you fail to act "like a human being," if you fail to do exactly what is expected of you, you get corrected on the spot loudly and perhaps embarrassingly, however you choose to take it.

"I'm not smart enough to use tact or to know how to say something nice," he would say. "I just tell 'em what the heck to do, that's all. If they play like human beings, I don't have to say anything."

But few athletes ever learned how to live up to Coach DV's definition of a human being. He always wanted more, expected more, demanded more; and the lessons he offered in the process were profound. What he imparted to a player was not only very meaningful, it was usually very colorful—a reporter's delight.

On several occasions, I remember him saying to me and to others, in total seriousness and with obvious anger: "Oh my, oh my, oh my! I have no idea what to even say about that. That is a *once-per-career mistake, and now you've had yours*! Don't *ever* do that again!"

Another time, with equal seriousness and almost paralyzing exasperation, Coach DV threw his hands in the air, looked up to the sky, and wheezed in the direction of his assistant coach, "I can't understand it, Jack, really I can't. I've been teaching this stuff for thirty-five years and they *still* haven't got it!"

Even he caught himself and laughed at that one, but he didn't laugh too often during practice. That's where he turned his simple, consistent philosophies into victories. "There's really nothing to coaching. It's the players that win games, not coaches. You can't win without the players. Let the other guys have all the tricky plays. I want the players.

"Once you've got your guys playing like basketball players, about all you can do is sit back and clap for them and cheer them on. There isn't that much a coach can do."

He sincerely thought that way. But I know from what I experienced and observed how very much he did and how rare it was. He reacted so naturally, so intensely, so unthinkingly, yet with so much common sense and single-minded purpose, it was truly an education playing for him. Generations of doctors and lawyers, guys in literally dozens of successful careers, will attest to the power of what he taught them as high school athletes.

In this book, I try to present his colorful principles and, in some cases, the methods—or antics—through which he delivered his philosophy to his teams. Some I explain at length. Others I leave to you to apply to your own life and way of thinking.

I feel sure, regardless of whom you are and what you do, that many of the principles will hit home with you immediately. Coach DV coached all kinds of players and rarely, if ever, had a kid who didn't respect him when the season was over. A lot had their difficulties at the time. My brother Huck led the world in verbal abuse from Coach DV. Nothing he did was ever right, although he was his high school's valedictorian. My brother Dave quit the team several times. I cried at practice nearly every day of my sophomore year and hated my father more times per day than I can count.

He never suspected those difficulties and barely even noticed their effects. There was a way to succeed—only one way—and he was going about it in the same way he did every day for forty years with every player he ever coached. That one way didn't leave time for noticing that a kid—his son or anyone else's—had hurt feelings or was winded or tired or depressed. There was only one way to win, and Coach DV, absolutely sure of what that way required, simply went to it—did it every day, without fail, without ever an ebb or flow or rise or drop in effort during forty years.

Someday, I would like to write a tribute to Coach DV, to his uncommon energy, to his ability, and to the special gift he gave to each player he coached throughout the years. But this book is not a gift to The Coach. It is a gift to you. I feel sure you will enjoy and benefit from Coach DV's lessons. I just hope I can do them justice and convey at least partially the impact they had on me and everyone else who played for him.

So I give you, without further embellishment, Coach DV. Because, as he so often said, "You gotta cut out all the talk and just go to work. There's only one way to win."

2.
THE BASICS

He really didn't do too much teaching. It was basically, fire you up, you do it. If you don't, you're out of there . . . On defense—and we prided ourselves on defense—he didn't teach you to extend your foot and split the man and take away the baseline. He just sort of said, "You just hunch on over and get up on his ass and you'll do all right."

— Coach Walt Ostrowski
Former Coach DV player

USUALLY, BEFORE HE HAD EVEN TOSSED A BALL TO ONE TEAM TO BEGIN PLAY, HE'D BE ANGRY. THAT LOOK OF TOTAL DISGUST AND ANGUISH WOULD COME OVER HIS FACE . . .

The Basics

To start practice or to start off a new season, some coaches go over a group of fundamental drills: dribbling, shooting, and passing. Groups of players get in lines and focus on one fundamental after another.

Coach DV would watch another coach do such things, and he would nod approvingly. "We should do more of that," he would say. But he never did much of it.

If his team members were nearby, he would grab them, even in the off-season, and he would be angry. "You see, boys, that's what you have to do. If you want to be a player, that's what you have to do. You have to put in the time; you have to make sure you can shoot and dribble and pass. You have to put in the time."

Nevertheless, he didn't spend time on shooting, dribbling, or passing. He thought players should do that on their own.

"You gotta put in time on your own, boys. You gotta be able to do what good players can do. There's no secret. If you want to be good, you have to practice. If you don't want to practice or put in time on your own, you should be doing something else. You have to decide what you want to do. If you want to play this game, then you have to play it. You have to eat, sleep, and dream it. That's if you want to be good. If you just want to participate, that's fine. But then you have to realize you're not a basketball player."

The need to practice diligently in the off-season was a rule that Coach DV wouldn't bother to articulate very often. It went without saying. Everyone knows that. If you want to be good at something, you watch players who are good. You see what they do and make sure you can do it, too. You find out how much time they spend and spend more than that amount of time.

That was merely stating the obvious, so Coach DV would

never think to state it at all—unless he was angry at a player who was playing poorly.

"You see, son, that's why you have to practice," he would say. "If you had put in the time, you would have taken that ball and dropped it in the basket, and I wouldn't be yelling at you now and your parents wouldn't have to call the school. Everybody would be clapping for you. I would be clapping for you, your parents would be clapping for you. They would think I was a great coach, and everyone would be happy. But now, no one is happy because you didn't practice. You have to practice."

Once the season began, Coach DV didn't feel there was time to spend on individual fundamentals. "Kids have to do that on their own. If they want to be good, they'll do it."

Coach DV's team fundamentals—the things he spent all of his time on—were ridiculously simple. To install his plan for the year, Coach DV didn't pass out any notebooks or distribute any handouts. If he saw some other coach doing that, he would say admiringly, "We ought to do that. I'd like to do that. That's a good idea. Players need to be reading things like that."

But Coach DV very seldom passed anything out. To install his plan for the year, Coach DV would get ten kids together and tell five of them to take their shirts off.

There usually wouldn't be many more than ten around. Why? "Because too many cooks spoil the soup," he liked to say. "You can't have too many kids on a basketball team—you'll just have problems." So he would discourage kids from coming out for the team. He wanted just the ones who had practiced.

Usually, before he had even tossed a ball to one team to begin play, he'd be angry. That look of total disgust and anguish would come over his face and everyone would get still.

Once, one kid had tossed his shirt off to the side and it hadn't gone completely off the court.

"Look, son," he said. "We can't play with a shirt on the court. You gotta act like a human being. What's wrong with you? Don't you see that out-of-bounds line? Don't you think that someone may soon be running or dribbling where that shirt is? You must be the dumbest man alive. Or maybe you can't see. I'm sorry. Have you had your eyes checked recently?"

You may think he was speaking sarcastically, but guess what? He was deadly serious. He couldn't believe that a person who could see clearly would throw a shirt on the court and just leave it there. No human being would do that!

"Son, do you watch pro games?" he continued. "You do? Good. How many pro games do you see that start with some shirts lying on the court? None? Well then what the hell—wait, excuse me, son, I don't want to yell bad words." [His voice would get soft now.] "Why would we want shirts on our court if the pros don't use them on theirs? C'mon now, son. Don't act like some dumb gazook. Act like a human being. That's all I ask. Just act like a human being. You don't throw a shirt on a court."

With five shirted players and five "skin" players, Coach DV would tell one team to "go that way" and he would toss a ball to one of the players.

Probably not more than a second or two later, Coach DV would be totally pissed off!

Either the kid who got the ball, one of the defenders, or someone else would be standing and watching.

"Son, you *never* stand on a basketball court," he would say. "Do you understand that? You never stand on a basketball court."

A youngster or someone inexperienced in the ways of Coach DV might proffer that the kid wasn't ready. He had expected a jump ball or one team to take the ball out of bounds in order to start the game.

"Son, look. You have to be ready. You have to always be ready. You see, son, this is a basketball court. When you step out here, you're ready. You're ready for anything. You're ready for the unexpected. You're ready for the expected. You're just ready for anything. And when something happens, you react. Never stand. Expect something to happen. You gotta . . ."

Coach DV would think he was getting through and then he'd look at the kid.

"No wonder you're not ready, you're standing there like a pregnant lady or an old fat man. You can't stand like that on a basketball court, son. Please, what are you trying to do? Look, you gotta stand like a basketball player. You bend your knees and you're ready to move to the left and to the right, you're ready to go backward and forward. You can't stand like a pregnant lady and play this game. C'mon, son, play like a human being. You gotta look like a basketball player."

Coach DV would put the ball back in play by handing it to a player. Never mattered which player, or which team had it last. The ball went to whomever he happened to give it to.

Sometimes, early in the season, an inexperienced player would stop and indicate, "It's our ball." Meaning that his team had possession of the ball back when Coach DV stopped the action to make a point.

Coach DV would erupt again, each time with equal or greater force than the last.

"Son, it's nobody's ball. This is basketball. It's a game. If you want the ball, you're always free to get it. You steal the ball, you rebound it, you play defense so close they have trouble breathing. It's not anyone's ball when I have it. What's wrong with you? Hasn't anyone ever taught you anything? C'mon, play."

The first time the ball actually advanced to one end of the court, a player would usually take it to the basket and score. Almost anyone who ever watched basketball would have the tendency to compliment some graceful or powerful dribbles into the basket and the shot that neatly bounced off the board into the basket: "Nice play! Nice shot!"

But not Coach DV.

"Gawt-darn-it!" he'd yell, walking out onto the court and making it clear with the look on his face that he wanted the ball and he wanted total silence and stillness.

"You can't just give away baskets. I know Carson played last year and he's supposed to be good, but you can't just let him score. He'll think he's All-American playing against you. You just *let* him go in there. You can't do that. You can't just *let* a guy score. You gotta get in front of him; you can't let him in there. You know where he wants to go, so just get there. You gotta play this game, you can't just stand around and watch and give away baskets. That's not sports. That's not basketball. That's Christmas. That's gift-giving. You do that on your birthday. Is it Carson's birthday?

"Excuse me, I'm sorry, Carson, is it your birthday?"

He would ask the question without a hint of sarcasm. Clearly, his mind would be off on the tangent. If by chance it were Carson's birthday, he would change his tone, and make it clear that he understood; it was okay. He would apologize for having gotten upset. But then he would make it abundantly clear: now that Carson has his gift, *you better not give him another*.

Of course, it typically wouldn't be Carson's birthday, and then Coach DV would be furious.

"What? It's not Carson's birthday? Well then what the hell are you doing? This is basketball. You can't just let a guy dribble the ball in like that and score an easy basket. You *never* give an easy basket. Never. This is my *life* you guys are playing with. If you don't want to play this game right, don't play it. Quit. You *never* give an easy basket."

Coach DV didn't think of these commands as being part of a philosophy of basketball. They were just common sense, a daily and constant part of every practice. He felt these ideas should go without saying. Every athlete or human being ought to know these things long before he ever went out for a basketball team.

But, was Coach DV just unlucky? No one ever came out for one of his teams with sufficient common sense to satisfy him. Coach DV's notion of common sense was a bit more stringent than anyone was used to. Few players practiced enough, few were ready for everything, and few were in the habit of never giving away opportunities to opponents. In other words, for forty years, even Coach DV's stars had to put in a great deal of time, not just practicing in the off-season, but in learning his meaning of common sense, how to be always ready, and how to make an opponent struggle for every dribble, pass, and shot.

What? Give 'em an easy basket? No way. And don't let them throw an easy pass. Don't let them dribble where they want to go. Don't let them run where they want to run. Make it difficult for them to breathe! *That* was basketball, Coach DV style.

That was the only way to win.

3.
PLAY LIKE A HUMAN BEING

I've played for a great many coaches but none was able to instill the fierce competitive spirit that you did. Maybe you didn't actually instill that in me, but believe me, Coach, you made me realize that it's the right and only way of going about things.

— Coach Ray Carion
Former Coach DV player

It's just entirely obvious. You have to go all out. That's the only way to do it. Anything less and you're simply being a horse's tail.

Play Like a Human Being!

The requirement to "play like a human being" was perhaps Coach DV's dominant theme. He always felt astonished that this concept required so much explanation. Coach DV felt that everyone understood what a human being ought to be like, how he ought to act, what he ought to do. Anything that fell short of that clear-cut concept was obviously out of line, repugnant, repulsive, annoying. It had to stop immediately. It could only be responded to with utter and instantaneous disdain.

Anything that was not what a human being would do brought practice to a stop on the spot. Didn't matter if the principal had just walked in or if cheerleader practice was going on or if the offender's parents were watching.

"You can't do *that*! Hold it. I said, *hold it!* Look, son, you can't do that. If you want to play basketball, you can't do that. *Never*. You can never do that. Do I need to speak Chinese so you can understand? Don't ever do that again."

What makes a subhuman? What made Coach DV tell a player just to act like a human being? Here are a few of the qualities that Coach DV considered essential parts of humanity.

1. Going All Out—Sprinting Instead of Trotting

"Trotting might be nice at a state fair or horse show," Coach DV once said, "but we don't have time for it here. This is basketball!"

Coach DV always assumed everyone knew that there is only one way on a basketball court to get from one place to another. You sprint. You go as fast as you can, 100 percent all the time. Anything less and you're obviously acting "like a goof." What could possibly make a kid think that you could beat anyone by trotting someplace? "Son, if you're gonna move like that, you are just letting the other team win. You can't just let another team win. You have to play them. You have to work. You have to go all out."

If you don't, in Coach DV's eyes, you're not even playing like a human being. Any human being should understand: in a basketball game, when there's only one ball for both teams, when both teams are trying to win, where there's a scoreboard and only one team can come out on top, you absolutely have to try harder than the other guy. If the other guy is going all out, you have to at least equal his effort. And you can never assume that you will equal another human being's effort unless you go all out. It's just entirely obvious. You have to go all out. That's the only way to do it. Anything less and you're simply being a horse's tail. That's abundantly clear. Everyone knows that, according to Coach DV.

2. Making it Tough on Opponents—and Getting a Hand Up on Defense

The other team has the ball. They want to score. Every player knows it is easier to score when there's no defender's hand in your face than when there *is* a hand in your face. It's so apparent, why would anyone even waste time saying it? If it's harder for them when a hand is in their face, then always put a hand in their face.

Coach DV would say, "You don't have to be Einstein to know that, do you?"

Translation: if the other team shoots and one of Coach DV's players failed to get a hand in their opponent's face, the player was a complete jerk. He was subhuman, just plain *giving* the game away. How could any human being go out for a team and then just *give* the game to the other team? There really isn't any other way to look at it, Coach DV figured. If there's something you can do that makes it more difficult for the other team, and if you're trying to beat that other team, then there's absolutely no choice at all. You either try to beat them by making it more difficult for them or you let them beat you by not doing that.

If you're a basketball player—if you're a human being—you will of course put your hand in every shooter's face every single time. It won't matter if you're ahead by 30, behind by 30, or the score is tied. "I'm not that smart," Coach DV would say. "I can't think that fast. It's easier for us dumb guys to just do what the heck you're supposed to do every time, and then you don't have to think. Why make the game hard? It's an easy game. You just have to do what you're supposed to do."

And you have to do it *every time*.

3. Being Ready to Move—Never Standing Straight Up

"Son, have you ever been in a fight?" Coach DV might say. "Have you ever watched good boxers box? Do you ever see them box a tough opponent with their knees straight? My gawd, you can't be ready to move with your knees straight. You gotta bend your knees.

"Haven't you ever watched a third baseman get ready for a pitch when a good hitter is at the plate? The guy has to be ready for a hot drive down the line or a grounder into the hole, and he has to be ready to run up for a bunt or back for a pop fly. Do you ever see a good third baseman stand straight up and wait? Of course you don't. You can't play sports like that.

"Have you ever seen a tennis star wait for a 120-mile-per-hour serve standing straight up? He has to be ready to go left, to go right. He has to decide everything in a split second. He *can't* do that standing straight up.

"And if the pros can't do those things standing straight up, why the hell would you think *you* could do it that way? That's ridiculous. Quit acting like a goof and get down like you're supposed to. Look like an athlete. Maybe you will fool some people. If you *look* like an athlete, maybe they won't know any better. They'll think you *are* one."

If that still wasn't clear, Coach DV would strain to control his exasperation. "Nice boy, nice friend, good boy, fine young lad, what do I have to do? Do I have to talk Chinese to you?"

Sometimes it would be "talk Chinese," sometimes "speak Chinese." Always it would be urgently expressed. It was not at all a slur against anyone from Asia. It was simply up and down instead of across; it was short, quick brush strokes instead of Petersen Directed Handwriting; it was hieroglyphics instead of words. It was totally different—like night and day—and it conveyed exactly what Coach DV meant when he was frustrated because a player's action made no sense to him.

Coach DV always wondered how it could happen that he could say something and make it crystal clear, and then, just a moment later, a kid would do something exactly the opposite.

"What do I need to do, speak Chinese? How could you have failed to understand that? Tell the truth, are you defying me? Are you trying to be a goof? Surely you know what I just said.

"If we had a lot of plays like other coaches, I could understand. But we don't have a lot of plays. I only ask you to do about four or five things. How can you possibly not do them?"

Coach DV was a master at keeping things simple. Usually, he didn't have to speak Chinese. His players understood him perfectly—or at least they understood perfectly that he was truly angry—just about all the time. If they weren't sure what they had done wrong, they could always fall back on the idea that they simply had failed to go all out.

"That's all I ask," Coach DV would say often, his head shaking in complete, confused sincerity. "Why do you have to make this great game seem so hard? Just play like human beings."

4.
MOOOOOVE!

He always seemed to be yelling and it never seemed to make any sense. But I was watching those old tapes, and you could hear Coach yelling at Billy and telling him to move and—it was amazing, I could see exactly what he meant. Billy should've been moving!

—Vernon Nelson
Former Coach DV player

A PLAYER ONCE SAID THAT A WHOLE CONSTRUCTION GANG OUTSIDE THE GYM ONCE CAME TO A COMPLETE, SILENT STOP WHEN THEY HEARD COACH DV YELL "HOLD IT!" INSIDE THE GYM . . .

MOOOOOVE!

One of the most obvious characteristics of highly successful people is that they know what they want; they know what is needed. They don't suffer from a lot of ambiguity when it comes to the essence of things.

For Coach DV, the essence of basketball could actually be encapsulated in just one four-letter word: M-O-V-E.

It was a word you could hear him bellow while still out in the parking lot if you arrived late for a game. His booming voice carried the brief message across even large arenas. This loud command jolted all five players at once and made the guys on the bench queasy—and maybe even the opponents! It was an urgent, incredibly forceful order. His players came to learn that precisely *where* they moved didn't matter. Coach DV wasn't that complicated. He didn't care where. He cared now. He cared fast. He cared quick.

"In basketball, you move," he would say. "You make it impossible for the other team to stay with you. You're here, you're there. You run hard. You stop fast, you start fast. You never stand. You never, never stand." Sometimes, he said it in a slightly different tone: "Son, this is a basketball game. Never stand in a basketball game. Move. *Move!* MOOOOOVE!" The word seemed to gather momentum as he strung it out—boomed it out!—and grabbed you with it.

To Coach DV, basketball is ridiculously simple. You move. The best players are the players who move best. Just watch an NBA game. Watch college. Watch high school. "There's no secret," he would say in a husky, admiring tone, while watching a good team at work, "they move."

You gotta move.

While most players and coaches would agree that movement

is important in basketball, few allowed it to dominate their view of the sport as Coach DV did. That's why most coaches' practice sessions are quite a different animal from one of Coach DV's practices.

The typical coach spends what Coach DV would consider an inordinate amount of time on things he could never find time for. But Coach DV was never critical of others. He never claimed their priorities were skewed. He had a healthy respect for all that goes into developing good basketball teams. Therefore, if he watched some other coach run a practice, he would invariably be impressed with all the things that coach was teaching and talking about. (Impressed, to an extent, but not at all in agreement with the priorities.)

If another coach ever asked him what he thought, Coach DV was always quick to say he was impressed. If pressed for specifics that might help correct a weakness, Coach DV would say he didn't want to get involved, that they had "some nice players" and he wished them well. It was hard to press him for an opinion because he found talk cheap. But if there was time, if the other coach was a friend or if the other coach was a young, sincere guy whom Coach DV decided truly wanted his help, then Coach DV came pouring out.

"Okay, boys, you seem like fine young men," he'd say, "and you seem like you want to play this game. I don't want to come in here and be critical, but if you want to play this game—I mean, your coach asked me to talk to you—and if you want to play this game, then you have to *play* it."

With that, he would stop everything they had been doing and go back to the basics, *his* basics—the essence. He would tell them they've got to *move*.

He would put them back in some lines he had seen and ask what they called that drill. "Four-corner passing? Okay, do four-corner passing again, only this time *move*!"

They wouldn't be into it more than three seconds before he would stop everything and call them back over.

"You see, boys, I don't want to holler and yell at you. I mean, you seem like good boys, but your coach here asked me to help you, and I can't help you if you're not gonna move. If you're gonna play basketball, you gotta move. When you come to meet the ball, you gotta *meet* the ball. When you're standing in line, you can't stand there like an old lady. You gotta be ready to move."

It never sounded particularly articulate. It *always* sounded particularly intense. The average coach just could not convey the sense of urgency that Coach DV could. Without even saying the words, Coach DV indicated that, this time, when he sent them back to run their four-corner passing drill, they needed to sprint to position, they needed to be moving around, talking, warning each other, getting each other ready, pushing, gesturing, screaming.

Anything done without a sense of urgency (more like desperation) was lackadaisical in Coach DV's mind, and nothing demonstrated that better than movement: the way players moved from place to place, the way they stood—fidgety at least!—in lines preparing for their turns. It didn't take Coach DV more than a second or two to notice if any team was "a real basketball team" or just a "group of nice boys"—impostors.

If he sent them back to do a drill again and they failed to show the urgency he wanted, there would be an immediate confrontation. There would have to be. There was no other way.

Typically, when such a situation occurred, Coach DV would bow out, telling the coach—again—that he didn't want to interfere. But if the coach prevailed on him and said please, then Coach DV would suddenly be livid, the way he *always* was during his own practices.

He would walk onto the court and make everything come to a complete halt. He could do it usually with just a glare, but he was willing to go as far as necessary. "Son, are you nuts? I'm about to talk." The implication was 100 percent clear. He didn't have to say the actual words very often. ("*You*, son, know absolutely nothing about this game. I may not be the greatest coach in the world. But you sure as hell ought to hang on every word I say.") They were to give him their total attention or get out right then. There was no other way.

A player once said that a whole construction gang outside the gym once came to a complete, silent stop when they heard

Coach DV yell *"Hold it!"* inside the gym. (Some of them had played for Coach DV, and they took his words seriously!)

"Son, now look, I don't want to have any problems with you. Do you want to play this game?"

It wasn't a rhetorical question. On Coach DV's own team, it could come accompanied by the coach's hand twisting the kid's shirt or grabbing the kid's arm, vice-like. Coach DV never hit a kid in his life, but his presence was very physical and commanding. It was nearly always enough for Coach DV just to stare down into a kid's soul. Few players ever encountered such intensity, so they had little problem recognizing the importance of the moment.

When the kid indicated that he did want to play basketball, then Coach DV went into an instant simmer, barely holding back an explosion which was just under the surface. Coach DV had not wanted to intrude, but once an agreement had been established—the kid said that he did indeed want to play the game—then there was no reason to hold back. There was only one way to play the game, and the kid wasn't doing it at all.

"Well, then son, if you want to play this game, you gotta *play* it. You gotta *move*. You gotta *work* . . . *Here's* the way you play basketball. You get down. No, *down*! And you're ready, and you move, you move. You're always ready to move. You go right, you go left, you go up, you go back. You're down, you're ready, you move. You move, son, you gotta *moooove*!"

If necessary, after demonstrating it himself and probably showing more intensity than the kid had ever seen, he pushed and pulled the kid back and forth to help him get the idea.

And then he complimented with the same intensity. "Yeah, that's it. You *can* do it. You see. You *do* understand. Now *that's* basketball. If you want to play this game, that's what you have to do. If you don't want to play it, then fine, do something else. But if you want to play this game, you gotta play it. You gotta move. Yeah. Now don't forget that, son. See, you *can* play this game—if you want to. And you say you want to, so you gotta do it now. You gotta move."

Nearly every coach's list of fundamentals was entirely different from Coach DV's "list." Coach DV's list wasn't really a list at all. It was a command. It was a *how,* not a *what*. The question wasn't what to do, but how to do it. It didn't much matter to Coach DV whether his team was dribbling or shooting or passing or playing defense. *How* were they going about it? Nothing really mattered until they learned *how*. The approach was everything, and there was only one way to win.

You gotta move!

5.
COACH DV'S FOUR RULES OF BASKETBALL

From what I read in the paper, it sounds as though you have the makings of another very good team, and I know you will bust their collective asses to make sure they reach their full potential.

—Tom Butler
Former Coach DV player

You know Tom there, sitting beside you. Tom, will you say hello to Joe-Joe-Bean here? Now, Joe-Joe-Bean, these are your teammates.

Coach DV's Four Rules of Basketball

Basketball coaches are typically fond of talking about all the things they do with their teams to get an advantage over other teams. Coach DV stayed out of these conversations. They irritated him.

"Coaches don't do anything," he would say. "Players do. They can have all the plays they want. I'll take the *players*. If you have good players, everything works; if you don't have good players, nothing works. There's no secret: you get good players and just play *bas*ketball. You don't need all that other crap."

At basketball camps and coaching clinics, he would often be asked by young coaches what his teams do.

"We don't do anything," he'd say. "We just try to play *bas*ketball."

Many interpreted his reply as a reluctance to give away secrets. But Coach DV really couldn't articulate what it was he did. Or, if he could, he wouldn't or didn't like to, or he was "tired of all this talk" and didn't even want to think about it.

Basically, his teaching consisted of four simple rules.

1. Always Move

Never stand. When in doubt, just run like hell. Without purpose? If need be! Move, move, move. Just keep moving and you'll be fine. Oh, and by the way, move fast. "Really move your fat tail. Don't shuffle around like some old lady. My grandmother could run faster than that. *Moooooove*!"

2. Always Throw the Ball to Your Own Team

Whenever he offered this rule at a clinic or to a coach, the response would be laughter, like, "Of course, everyone knows that. There he goes again, the colorful old coach, claiming one of his basics is to throw the ball to your own team." That was indeed one of his four rules, and it was not said for amusement. He could get immediately irritated just thinking about it, which is why he tried diligently to keep from getting in discussions with coaches. Had he told any coach what he was really thinking, it would have gone something like this:

"Yeah, you laugh like 'everyone knows that' but the problem is, I've seen your teams play. You got all those offenses and special plays, and then your team gets in a game and meets some kids playing good defense and your guys throw the ball to the wrong team. That's how you lose games, throwing the ball to the other team. *You can't throw the ball away!"*

He just hated throwing the ball away without getting a chance to score. Not only was there an opportunity for points lost, but throwing the ball to the other team usually resulted in their getting an easy opportunity before a defense could be set.

"When you throw the ball away, it makes everything you do wasted. [And it makes all that coaching talk a joke.] You spend half your time on defense—but you don't even get a chance to get back to play defense if you throw the ball to them—and you spend the rest of your time on scoring, and you don't get a chance to score if you throw the ball away. You just *can't* throw the ball away.

"The ball is 20-carat gold. You gotta guard it with your life."

In a state championship game, midway through the final quarter, our team—Coach DV's undefeated team—led by 35 points (*35 points* over another undefeated team!), and I threw two consecutive passes away. Coach called an immediate timeout and was furious. He growled and screamed into the towel bunched up in his hand and then stuck his finger an inch from my face, screaming in total anger, completely serious: "If it wasn't for you, we could've broken this game wide open!"

He laughs about that comment now, but it wasn't at all funny at the time. He was furious. You *never* throw the ball away.

3. Take Only Very Easy Shots

Another laugher. Everyone knows it's good to take easy shots. But again, the problem is that in games, coaches don't require it and teams don't do it. They take difficult and bad shots.

"They just *throw* the ball at the basket. You can't just throw the ball at the basket. You look like you're trying to knock the rim down or break the board. You can't just throw it up there. You gotta *put* it in."

The idea is to move fast and pass to each other until someone gets an easy shot that anyone can make. Coach DV didn't want anyone making difficult shots. He wanted all the shots to be easy.

When a player would make a shot and run back hearing the applause and show pride in his achievement, Coach DV would be quick to criticize. "Don't run back like you did anything. Anyone can make an easy shot. Little kids could make that shot. Hell, my grandma could make that shot."

It was the pass and the movement that created the opportunity *That* was what deserved the applause, Coach DV said, not the shot itself.

Long before legendary North Carolina coach Dean Smith started his now world-renowned practice of having his players point at the passer in order to thank him, Coach DV was ordering his players to thank each other. He didn't require a public acknowledgment, but he did require that his players thank each other. And he growled away any player's swagger after scoring a basket. Coach DV always complimented the passer in hoarse yells that could be heard across the gym. He just loved a great pass.

"*He* got that basket, not *you*! Next time you act like that, he's not going to pass to you, and I won't blame him. He'll fake the pass to you and shoot himself. Who the hell do you think you are? Anyone could make that shot. Thank the guy who gave you the ball. *That's* who scored the basket. Anyone can make an easy shot."

4. Never Give the Other Team an Easy Shot

This was Coach DV's one rule that covered everything he

really cared about on defense. Did defense take a backseat for him? Hardly. He spent half his time on it. But he wasn't interested in a lot of "rigmarole."

"Get your man and get on him."

When he would call a timeout because the other team was suddenly scoring some baskets, he was unlikely to change defenses. He was a lot more likely to succinctly review each player's assignment.

"Who's your man? Well then get him!"
"Who's your man? Well then get him!"
"Who's your man? Well then get him!"
"Who's your man? Well then get him!"
"Who's your man? Well then get him!"

Just a lot of foolish repetition? It never seemed like it. In fact, as he went to each player, perhaps grabbing the kid's shirt for emphasis and looking him dead in the eye from just a few inches away, each question seemed to come with complete, spontaneous inspiration. When he stared at the kid and asked the question, the kid had only one thing on his mind: to tell Coach the name and number of the player he was guarding and to nod that he sure as hell was going to get him.

"You *can't* give your man an easy basket. If he makes a tough shot, I'll take the blame for it. I'll take the blame for all of those. But not easy ones. You can't give them any easy ones. If you do that, you might as well just give them the game. What's the point of playing if you aren't going to make it tough for them? They won't even want to play you. And they won't respect you after the game if you're just gonna let 'em score. *You can't let 'em score. You gotta make them work for everything they get.*"

"Coach, do you want me to have my right foot forward or my left foot forward when I guard a player along the baseline?"

"I don't care what's forward. Just get down like a basketball player and don't let him go by you. Get on him!"

When someone did score an easy one for the other team, they could expect to hear it again: *"Get on him!"*

"But Coach, that wasn't my man."

But Coach? A kid could get away with that only once in his career with Coach DV. There weren't any *But Coach*es. A player free to score an easy basket was *everybody's* man. And when Coach yelled, it was clear to everyone that it was everyone's responsibility. At the time, the mere power of the yell would make it clear. But later, in a somewhat quieter tone (at least initially), Coach DV would explain it with sarcasm appropriate to absolute catastrophe.

"Son, this is a *team*. Will you please look around you? You know Tom there, sitting beside you. Tom, will you say hello to Joe-Joe-Bean here? Now, Joe-Joe-Bean, these are your teammates. They are on your team. This is us, this group here, this is our team. During games, we play other teams. You see the scoreboard up there? It just says *Us* and *Them*. This is *Us*. There isn't anything up there that says Joe-Joe-Bean. It's just *Us*. We play games. And we try to win games. And when someone scores on *Us*, Joe-Joe-Bean, they score on our *team*. So there isn't any such thing . . . I don't know where you came up with this crap. Have you been reading some new book or something? 'Cause we don't have that stuff here. We just have this group of guys. This is our team, and when they score on us, they put two more points up on that scoreboard—and we all lose, Joe-Joe-Bean. Do you understand that? If you want to play games by yourself, you have to play tennis or golf. I don't have anything against tennis or golf. Those are good games. I like those games. But this is basketball. It's a team game. When they score on one of us, they score on all of us, so it's always your man, Joe-Joe-Bean. Do you understand this? 'Cause I can't stop and explain this to you each time someone scores. I just can't play you. 'Cause you can't let the other team just score. Then it's not even a sport. You gotta make them work for everything they get."

Coach didn't give that speech very often. Only about once a year. The kid's name, of course, was not Joe-Joe-Bean! But the message got through loud and clear. Usually, however, Coach DV's intensity got the same message across without actually articulating the whole speech.

Man-to-man, zone, or his famous matchup defense—the actual method defense didn't matter too much to Coach DV. It was the way the defense was played, and the basic rules for all of his defenses were about the same: don't give 'em anything easy. Whether a player was guarding an area on the court or guarding a particular man, the same basic requirements prevailed: never let a shooter shoot without a hand in his face, never let a ball be passed to someone near the basket, and never let a guy dribble in for a lay-up.

"You tackle him first if you have to," he'd say, "but you never let a guy dribble in for a lay-up. *All five of you tackle him if you have to*. You can't give lay-ups. If you're gonna do that, you might as well not even play the game. First graders can shoot lay-ups. How can you ever expect to win if you let the other team shoot lay-ups?"

But what about 3-pointers? How did the old-fashioned coach react to the rule-change that allowed them? It didn't change his coaching style at all.

"Of course a kid can make 3-pointers, if you let him shoot. Little fat kids can make shots if no one's on 'em. Everyone can shoot nowadays. A lot of these kids have baskets in their backyards. Of course they can shoot—if you let 'em just stand there. But you can't let a kid just *stand* there and shoot. You gotta get on 'em. Not many kids can shoot when you're on 'em."

So there you have it. Coach DV's remarkable rules of basketball. Hardly a clinician's dream. Move, pass to each other, shoot easy shots, and don't let the other team shoot any easy shots.

Doesn't sound like much. Just the basis for forty consecutive years of winning seasons!

6.
CRAP, IMPATIENCE, VISION, PARENTS, PIANOS, FAIRNESS, AND LIFE ITSELF

My kids are in high school and they both really like Coach DV. I always thought you had to be out of school for ten years before you could appreciate that sonofabitch!

— Mike Onufer
Former Coach DV player

THE CLARITY OF HIS VISION WAS WHOLE, INTEGRAL. THE PIECES FIT TOGETHER SO OBVIOUSLY, IT WAS DIFFICULT FOR HIM TO SEPARATE INDIVIDUAL PARTS IN ORDER TO EXPLAIN THEM.

Crap, Impatience, Vision, Parents, Pianos, Fairness, and Life Itself

The true winners in life, as in sports, always seem to be people who are extremely impatient with anything less than perfection. Certainly Coach DV falls into that category, but he wouldn't think of it in quite those terms. He would, however, readily admit to being extremely impatient with any kind of crap.

"Don't gimme that crap," he'd say.

He hated crap. He hated anything that didn't directly contribute to winning and losing basketball games. That would include meddlesome parents, paperwork, meetings with administrators, and a variety of other everyday events. For example:

Most basketball players love throwing up "crazy shots" before practice begins. Most coaches are not equally thrilled. For Coach DV, it would take only one to set him off.

"Hold it. *Hold the ball!*"

When he bellowed out an angry command, the air itself seemed to get still. The girls practicing cheerleading or painting signs in the lobby beyond the gym doors would stop. Some kid had done the unthinkable—a sophomore no doubt—had thrown up a left-handed hook shot from the corner.

"Cut that crap. We don't have time for that crap here. Go somewhere else and do that—on your own time, not on my time."

The kid undoubtedly thought he *was* shooting on his own time, before practice had begun, when some other players still hadn't arrived yet. But no time was the appropriate time to shoot crazy shots if Coach DV was in sight.

"Son, when you're as good as Oscar Robertson, *then* you can shoot those shots. But you're not Oscar Robertson, you're Heininger. You can barely walk, you poor simp. You don't have time to shoot those shots, don't you see that? You still have trouble with lay-ups."

Usually after a speech like this, he would walk away muttering loud enough for anyone nearby to hear, "How can anyone be so *gawt*-darn dumb?"

He honestly couldn't understand it. How could a kid having trouble with lay-ups not realize that he needed every minute of every day—plus a lot of minutes that no longer existed—just to approach adequacy?

Watching one of those shots disgusted Coach DV sincerely and thoroughly. The kid, invariably, would wonder what all the fuss was about, but he would be very unlikely to shoot any more crazy hook shots if he thought Coach DV was anywhere nearby.

Great coaches, and probably great people in all walks of life, have a clear idea of what is required for success. The extraneous things which the rest of us do routinely—things which do not lead to success or add to it in any way—are therefore irritating to those few who understand what it takes to succeed. Focused people have a vision that most of the rest of us lack. We tend not to think that a hook shot thrown up before practice could possibly be bad, especially when some other players are not even on the court yet.

Parents could become irate over that kind of issue but Coach DV rarely, if ever, explained his thinking to any of them. He didn't look upon himself as having some special vision and understanding. He gave himself credit, at most, for just a little common sense. He would tell those parents, if confronted, that their son simply didn't have time for hook shots. Such shots were crap that was standing in the way—directly in the path—of success. Couldn't they see that?

But no, they couldn't see that. After all, their son had taken *only one hook shot* and this insane coach had blown up and made fun of their son *in public*.

(What the hell would public or private have to do with it?

Coach DV would wonder. He would never understand that one. In fact, he would never get around to even considering that issue among all the other ones. How could parents think so differently? They made no sense at all to Coach DV.)

The parents might call the principal or athletic director with what seemed like an entirely appropriate accusation: "What about the other kids who weren't even there? At least their son, the hook shooter, had taken some good shots, hadn't he? In fact, he had taken dozens of good shots when the other players weren't even out of the dressing room yet. How could one hook shot be so criticized? This coach must be insane."

Coach DV would find reasoning like that utterly ridiculous, and he would be much too impatient to search for the words that would convey the reasoning behind his outburst. He would usually just get furious. *Couldn't they see*?

The clarity of his vision was whole, integral. The pieces fit together so obviously, it was difficult for him to separate individual parts in order to explain them, and it was difficult for him to understand that others didn't see the obvious as clearly as he did. Often, he just thought they were being "funny" (trying to be contentious). How could parents even *think* about wasting his time and calling the school, talking about unfair treatment of their son? How could they miss what was really at issue? If they were so dumb as to call the school with an accusation, they were certainly too dumb to understand the real issue.

What Coach DV would have said—if he could have gotten out the words—was this: "If your son were out here first everyday, shooting diligently and working on his game, of course I wouldn't mind him shooting one hook shot. Hell, I would let him shoot hook shots *in the games*! But that's not your son. Your son isn't diligent. He doesn't out-practice all of the others. He doesn't shoot more shots than any of them. The fact that he happened to be in the gym before the others this particular time was nothing but pure happenstance. Your son doesn't come to the gym determined to maximize his time. *You* haven't taught him that yet."

It was far beyond the scope of a coach to tell a man and a woman they were bad parents, but in Coach DV's mind, they were absolutely ridiculous to call the school and question the treatment their son got when, if they actually knew anything about good parenting, they would have criticized their son themselves. They would have been doing it consistently over the past fifteen years so that an incident like this could never even come up.

Real parents, Coach DV thought, guided their kids and helped them learn respect, helped them understand that when someone does you a favor (like keeping you on a team when your abilities are marginal) it's your job to bend over backwards to repay the kindness. Coach DV could even understand parents not teaching their kids to maximize their time, but how could they let their kids crap around and undermine their own chances for success and then go to bat for them when someone tried to straighten them out and help them? Parents, Coach DV thought, were simply the dumbest, blindest, most irrational people in the world when it came to their children.

"I'm sorry," DV would say, "but that's just the way I feel. I've seen it over and over again. Over the course of the season, there is only limited time to improve. Some days, some kids will have time or make time to come to practice early to try to improve before practice begins. Other days, other kids will have or make time.

"One hook shot is not the issue. It's what that hook shot tells me. It tells me that he doesn't yet understand. He takes 500 fewer shots than the others every week, and the others are already better than he is. Even *they* don't take enough shots, but your son doesn't understand that he has to work every second to try to catch up. He has to realize that he's here on borrowed time. Hell, my son used to shoot 5000 extra shots every week. That's what good players do.

"But I don't want to go into all that. I'm not saying that your son should shoot 5000 shots per week. Not everyone needs to be a basketball player. There are plenty of wonderful things to do in the world. I never said basketball was crucial to anyone's life. But, in your son's case, I didn't criticize him for the sake of basketball. I tried to help him. A kid like that has to understand that he is on this team by a thread. He just barely made it. We gave him a chance. We hoped he would catch on. We knew he had a lot going against him. But we hoped he would begin to understand.

"It doesn't matter that it's basketball. It could be piano lessons. You don't beg a piano teacher to take on one more student—her worst student, below her typical standards—and then expect that piano teacher to sit across the room calmly, before a lesson begins, and listen to that kid bang the keys with his elbows. It's not that the kid at the keyboard doesn't excel in music. If he's banging on the keyboard with his elbows, he's showing that he doesn't understand life!"

Can you imagine a coach giving that speech to every parent who ever questioned an incident? It would be impossible even if the coach could articulate all of those ideas without interruption. But of course, there were always interruptions. And Coach DV would never claim to be articulate enough to say all that, anyway. About the only claim he ever made was that he understood what it took to win basketball games.

He understood, in fact, the essence of sports and of life, intuitively and instinctually. He didn't have to think about it—and didn't very often. It was just obvious.

Chuck DeVenzio grew up during the Depression. Times were very tough. He came from a large family, and many days there was very little to eat. He had older brothers who wouldn't mind swatting a little kid who stepped out of line. He learned to appreciate value and hard work. There was no other way. There wasn't time for any crap. Survival was at stake, and those lessons never left him.

You didn't toss up hook shots in front of a man who had given his life to basketball and to the values that could be learned from the sport. Coach DV would never have thought to express to a principal or some parents that he took his life and others' lives seriously; that he didn't believe in frivolity where diligence was required; that for him a basketball court was a sacred place. Or more precisely, basketball was life itself. He couldn't just sit back calmly, anymore than that virtuoso piano teacher could let her piano be profaned by the elbows of a kid just playing around, banging away. Coach DV couldn't sit back calmly and watch life be profaned by a kid carelessly tossing up a hook shot on a basketball court. It wasn't just a shot, it was life itself.

7.
BLUNTNESS, SENSITIVITY AND —TUNGO, TUNGO, TUNGO— A HAND IS A THING!

Congratulations! What a sensational story and storybook year! Even up here in Connecticut you have impressed the young bucks as you became a legend. I have newspaper articles plastered all over my office. Also, thank god for USA Today—it kept me up with things. Although this is my thirtieth year of teaching and coaching, none of it compares with what you have accomplished. I'm so proud of you and what you have done. There are no words to describe the inspiration one feels. It makes me want to go on and on, to keep living life one day at a time to the fullest.

— Coach Rick Osvick
Former Coach DV player

Coach DV's "Play ball!" was hardly that hearty, happy sound of an umpire's voice ringing out and signaling the beginning of a baseball game. It was, instead, a deep guttural sound.

Bluntness, Sensitivity, and— Tungo, Tungo, Tungo— A Hand is a Thing!

Some people would call it being blunt, but Coach DV didn't have names or too many thoughts about his personal ways of doing things. He just did what came naturally and, when it came to correcting an error, he simply did what every good referee tries to do: he calls 'em as he sees 'em.

Here's a colorful sampling of his frequently used expressions; You goof. Quit acting goofy . . . What are you, some kind of nut! . . . My grandma can run faster than that . . . You look like a pregnant lady . . . Why do you have to have that egg up your tail?. . . If you'd take the egg outta your tail, you could run like a basketball player . . . You poor simp . . . My heart bleeds for you . . . You know, you're no basketball player . . . You're no dribbler . . . You're no shooter . . . Holy hell, nobody's that good, what the hell are you doing? Have you gone completely crazy? . . . You can't trail a man like a caboose . . . You went by way of New Castle . . . You gotta cut him off at the pass . . . Don't you ever watch any of those old cowboy movies? . . . You can't just let a guy go right in there . . . You're running behind him like an old fat lady . . . No, hell, any fat lady could play better defense than that . . . What's wrong with you, Joe-Joe-Bean? You look like dead fish at the fish market . . . Have you ever seen dead fish just staring? . . . You don't have to actually laugh but at least look alive . . . My aunt could get more rebounds just standing there. You're allowed to go after the ball . . . Wait, excuse me—I'm sorry, no, I mean it—did someone tell you not to go after the ball? . . . What? No? Then, gawt-darn-it, Joe-Joe-Bean, go after it! You can't just stand there and watch; this is my life you're fracking with . . . Cut the crap and play ball!

On paper, many of his comments sound heartless and uncaring, but Coach DV didn't want to hurt anyone's feelings. He never considered hurting feelings. It was not a matter of hurting feelings. It was just talking, communicating, telling it like he felt it.

Coach considered himself extremely sensitive. "I cry easily," he would say, "and things bother me more than others."

"You? Sensitive?" someone might ask.

"Oh yeah, extremely much so," Coach would answer, with total sincerity.

"Then how could you call that kid a fat ass? Did you think that wasn't going to hurt his feelings?"

"I wasn't trying to hurt his feelings. But what else could I say? He *was* a fat ass—I mean, he was playing like one. I never really thought about it. He was playing like a fat ass, so I called him one. I think he knew I wasn't trying to hurt his feelings."

The kid didn't. But he—and forty years of players, of all shapes and sizes—realized that there was only one way to win Coach DV's respect and keep from being called any number of names that could indeed hurt feelings: hustle and work, strive and fight, and show every minute that you were willing to give your heart and soul to basketball. Anything less was unacceptable, and he spared no one. Stars, majorettes walking through the gym, or assistant coaches. Coach DV called 'em as he saw 'em.

Coach DV's assistant of ten years, Al Turley, usually stood beside him in pre-practice meetings in front of the team. Coach would go over the previous game, the practice to come, and the general state of affairs as he saw them. He did this daily and usually asked Turley if he had anything to add before practice began. One day, Coach DV explained something in his usual intense way, then paused for a moment. Taking the pause as a cue, Turley said, "In other words, boys, what Coach means is this: you've got to . . ." Before Turley could finish, DV interrupted, furious: "Bullshit, Abs," he said. "I meant what the hell I just said!"

Later, he would apologize to Turley. He never intended to be abrupt or insensitive or derogatory. He just had an intense dislike for wasting time and for obscuring the essence of things. When he felt that was happening, he had to cut it off. He felt you just couldn't win if you tolerated crap. There was only one way to win, and it didn't include a bunch of crap.

One of Turley's favorite aspects of the game—his specialty you might say—was underhand free-throw shooting. Coach DV let him be the "free throw shooting specialist" because DV personally didn't have much interest in shooting. His philosophy was very simple: basketball players were going to shoot well in the games if they were willing to practice hard in the off-season. If they were not willing to practice hard in the off-season, no amount of coaching was going to make much difference. "You can't *coach* good shooting," Coach DV believed. "A player has to become a good shooter through practice."

So Turley was his free throw shooting specialist. The problem was, when he sent Turley to a basket to help a kid on free throws, Coach DV would look down there after a few minutes and often Turley would be shooting! "See, see," Turley would add from time to time, showing the kid over and over what to do as he (Turley) worked to get into "the rhythm."

Soon, Coach DV would bellow down the court, "*Gawt*-darn-it, Abs! If I wanted *you* to practice free throws, I would've sent you down there alone!"

Coach DV wasn't shy about saying—out loud so he could easily be heard by anyone including assistant coaches—that assistant coaches were a necessary evil. You needed them around some time in case you got called away or got sick or something (which Coach DV *never* did) but basically, any head coach could get more accomplished once he had figured out a way to get his assistant to shut the hell up. He didn't really feel that way one hundred percent (he knew that assistants could be useful, and he had long, happy relationships with several assistants), but he wanted to keep them on their toes to make sure they didn't obscure the things he wanted to emphasize.

Coach DV was always aware that there was only so much a kid could learn in a day, and assistant coaches had the exasperating habit, he thought, of clouding the issues by adding too much explanation about things that were unimportant or flat-out wrong.

"Put your right foot forward and balance your shoulders over your knees," his assistant might say.

"*Gawt*-darn-it, Abs! I don't give a crap what's forward or where the hell his shoulders or knees are. Tell 'im to get off his fat tail and play ball. That's all he has to do. Quit confusing him with a bunch of crap. He's just gotta decide to play ball!"

After a comment like that, DV would often blow the whistle, gather the whole team together, and start out quietly:

"You see what you're doing, boys. I'm standing here yelling at my own assistant, Mr. Turley here, and I'm feeling bad, and he's feeling bad, and he's just trying to help you. I'm sorry, Abs, I know you were trying to help the kid, and it was probably good instruction, but dammit, we don't have time for good instructions if you guys aren't gonna play ball. Now get down, and get ready, and play ball. I've had enough of this shittin' around. *Play ball!*"

Coach DV's "Play Ball!" was hardly that hearty, happy sound of an umpire's voice ringing out and signaling the beginning of a baseball game. It was, instead, a deep guttural sound that came from somewhere deep in his soul. It had a toughness and an intensity that literally scared everyone.

When Coach DV said he was "tired of this crap, now play ball," it was as if he were standing over each player with his fingers stuck between their shoulder blades, pushing them from place to place. Players might continue to make mistakes, but the effort was *always* there. Once the effort was clearly in place, the rest of the instruction could go on—and it would because DV found something that disgusted him every ten seconds, or less.

"Hold it, hold it, *hold the ball!*" he would shout.

The gym would come to a stop. Everyone was quiet and still. No one shuffled around or shifted positions when Coach DV was mad.

"Look, boys, I don't want to keep hollering at you. You're trying hard, and I appreciate that. I really do, but you can't play like a bunch of screaming ninnies. Now look, this is basketball. Tungo, tungo, tungo. We don't have to do anything crazy or spectacular. Look. You just throw it to him, and you throw it to him. Yeah, that's it, just play nice, help each other. Me to you, to him, to him, back to me, over to him. It's not hard, don't make it so hard, boys. It's just tungo, tungo, tungo."

Tungo, tungo, tungo—even Coach DV didn't know why—just meant the ball went snappily but uneventfully from one player to another. No fancy dribbles, no clever maneuvers. Just catch the ball and throw it immediately to a teammate.

But his idea of tungo, tungo, tungo wasn't as easy for players to do as he thought it ought to be.

"Look, son," he would say. "See this? This is a *hand*. Yeah, it is. This is a hand. Now look at it. You see it, don't you? Five fingers. Four fingers here and a thumb here. It's a hand. You know it's a hand, don't you? Good. Well, son, a hand is a thing. It's a thing, son. You can't throw a ball through a thing. You see, son?"

He would jam the ball against his hand again and again and then grab the kid's hand and jam the ball once or twice into the kid's hand.

"Do you understand, son? It's a hand. A hand is a thing. You can't throw a ball through a thing. You have to throw over it or under it or around it. You can't throw a ball through a hand."

Coach DV wondered if he somehow hadn't been emphatic enough. Was there something he had failed to communicate? There must have been, he thought; otherwise, kids wouldn't keep trying to throw balls through hands.

"Boys, I appreciate you working hard. You're trying, you really are. I don't like hollering at you, but if you work hard, you can't turn it all to crap by throwing the ball right into a hand. *Miss* the hand, miss the hand. Do you understand?"

It was hard for him not to be constantly frustrated. His grandma, he always assured everyone, would never try to throw a ball through a hand. Why do sixteen-year-old boys try it so often? Basically, he thought the instruction required for basketball was a lot like that needed for learning to ride a bike. "You just gotta go out and do it."

Someone could tell you all sorts of things, but you had to do it yourself: make mistakes, learn from your mistakes, and just keep at it. That's why he hollered so much. "If you don't tell them at the time, and if you don't make it emphatic, how are they going to learn?"

8.
BLAMING THE BEST

I have two kids at home and, like most people with kids, I worry about them all the time. Since they [were] born, I prayed for them each day, not for Olympic gold medals or NCAA titles or that they become medical doctors. I pray to god for just one thing: that someday, somewhere along the way into each of their lives will walk their own personal Coach DV. And the day god answers that prayer is the day I won't worry about my kids anymore.

— Dr. Warren Ferguson
Former Coach DV player

I shouldn't have to yell at you, Johnson, but if we don't have Bird on our team, then you can't play like we have Bird on our team. We haven't had Bird all year. Forget about Bird. This is Jones.

Blaming the Best

Literally thousands of times in Coach DV's illustrious career, he shocked his star player by "jumping in his face" when one of the other players—not the star—made a mistake which enabled the opponent to score. The exchanges that occurred, when they came during games, shocked the fans, too.

A mediocre player would allow his man to penetrate to the basket for an easy shot, or some other player would throw an obviously bad pass that would sail out of bounds. At times like those, it was typical for fans to look at Coach DV to see his reaction. Would the kid be yanked from the game?

Many fans used to say that the real enjoyment of the games came just from watching Coach DV's antics and emotional reactions. Coach DV wouldn't hesitate to pull a starter from a game in favor of an untried junior varsity player. He'd stick Kruth in the game, and the fans would groan.

"He's just crazy enough to do something good in there," Coach DV would say about a kid who hadn't even played particularly well for the jayvees. Although the fans and even his assistant coach would disagree completely with the decision, the kid would almost always do something good. Coach DV's instincts were nearly as infallible as his willingness to try the unexpected. Fans just never knew what Coach DV would do.

Following obvious errors by teammates, it wasn't unusual for a star to look over to Coach DV (at least early in a season, before he learned) perhaps as if to ask, "What can we do?" or at least to get reassurance that whatever had happened wasn't his fault.

But those looks, instead of being rewarded with reassurance, were often met with scowls of disgust. Coach DV's response was always instantaneous. He could spot a mistake coming long before it actually happened. Usually long before the star had time to seek reassurance, Coach DV was yelling at him, pointing, and telling him in the most precise terms: "*You* threw that pass!"

Or in the case of the easy basket: "*You* just gave them that basket!"

"Who me?" the kids might reply. "I didn't throw that pass." Or, "I was all the way on the other side of the court. I didn't give them that basket."

Few players actually spoke up and voiced their objections, however. Mostly they just felt hurt and bewildered. Maybe they were furious. *They* didn't do anything wrong.

But Coach DV was adamant and always entirely clear in what he thought, even if much less clear in what he said. What had happened was so obvious to him that spelling it out seemed unnecessary. He believed his criticism was the only reasonable explanation for the error.

"*You* just gave them that basket!"

Only occasionally did he explain: "Any poor simp could have seen that their kid was going to take the ball to the basket. He takes it just about every time he gets the ball. And poor little Jones was guarding him. Didn't you *see* that was Jones? Who has Jones *ever* stopped? That wasn't Michael Jordan guarding the ball. That was Jones. You know everyone flies by Jones."

Usually then, Coach DV would pause and look over at Jones. "I don't mean to yell at you, Jones. You're trying, you're working at it. But you don't stop anyone."

"We didn't need a *gawt*-darn soothsayer to know that guy was going to take the ball to the basket. What the hell could you have been thinking?" Coach DV would scowl again at the star. "You're at practice every day. You know Jones can't stop anyone. How was he gonna stop that kid on their team? You were standing right there, just a few feet away, and it was like, every person in the stands knew that kid was going to pass Jones up and go to the basket. *You* were the only person in the building that had no idea what the hell was going on.

"I can't yell at Jones. He's trying. He's just too small and too weak. He hasn't learned how to play this game yet. But you," Coach pointed and scowled at the star again, "*You* know how to play this game, you're just too *gawt*-darn dumb or too *gawt*-darn lazy—I'm not sure which it is. You *had* to see that guy was going to take the ball in. Couldn't you see that?"

Hard to believe that what seemed so incredibly illogical to so many players for so many years was actually so incredibly logical. When a star, capable of anticipating a play and preventing it, failed to do that, it was indeed his fault. It was that simple.

And when that bad pass went sailing far over the star's head, clearly making it the passer's fault in every fan's eyes, Coach DV would often launch into another one of his furious tirades:

"*You threw* that pass!"

The star would think, Who *me*? I was waiting to *catch* it. What game are you watching? That ball flew six feet above my head into the ninth row of the bleachers."

But Coach DV was relentless. "Yes, you. You threw it away just as though you had grabbed the ball yourself and kicked it out of bounds."

Was Coach nuts? How could he say such a thing?

Easy! But again, the explanation, so rarely stated, was so obvious in retrospect.

"The grade school cheerleaders could see Jones was in trouble," Coach DV would say. "Hell, he was shaking like a leaf—I'm sorry Jones, I don't mean to yell at you, but if you want to learn to play this game, you're going to have to lift weights all summer and practice hard and learn to play this game. You've got to learn to play this game—But *you*!" Coach DV turned back to the star. "You *saw* that was Jones. You *saw* him about to pee in his pants. You *saw* that double-team, and you *knew* Jones was shaking like a leaf. Poor, nice Jones. You *knew* he couldn't wait to get rid of the ball, and you *just stood there* waving your arms like a *gawt*-darn *flagman*!

"Did you think that was Bird? Bird doesn't play on our team. I know you're a fan and you like the Celtics. That's nice. But you're not playing with the Celtics. When you play with the Celtics, you can stand in the corner and be a flagman. You can stay the hell out of the way and if Bird wants you to have the ball, he can throw it to you once in a while. But this is Jones. Look at him. You see him every day in practice. This is poor little, nice little kid Jones. *Gawt*-darn-it, when Jones gets the ball, you have to be ready to run right up to him and take it off him. And Jones, you just gotta lift some weights and get tougher and learn how to play this game. But 'til Jones does that—we can't wait 'til Jones does that. Jones may never do that. Dammit, Jones! Are you gonna get stronger or am I gonna have to yell at Johnson here every time you get the ball? Hell, I shouldn't have to yell at you, Johnson, but if we don't have Bird on our team, then you can't play like we have Bird on our team. We haven't had Bird all year. Forget about Bird. This is Jones. When Jones gets the ball, run up to him so he can hand it to you, do you understand? You're no passer, Jones. When you get the ball, just hold it until you can give it to somebody. Dammit, if only I had a couple of kids that could play this game, it would be so easy. They're just *letting* you guys have easy baskets and you won't take them."

Coach DV had an acute sense of what was going to happen—a terrific sense that made everything so clear to him, he just couldn't help but be disgusted with anyone who failed to see the obvious the way he did. When a player failed to react to something so apparent, Coach could attribute it to nothing other than laziness or falling asleep, which is why he would often yell after a mistake: *wake up*!

How could a star fail to get his body in the lane to stop a penetration that even the grade school cheerleaders could see was coming? How could a star fail to run toward a kid who was an inch away from peeing in his pants? There could only be one explanation: the kid had fallen asleep.

"Wake up, Johnson," he'd say. "You're just giving them this game!"

It hadn't initially seemed like Johnson's fault, but it was. Johnson had been capable of doing something to prevent the error, but hadn't reacted. Coach DV's thinking, once understood, was quite logical. Why bother yelling at the referee or at some little kid who just couldn't get the job done in spite of trying hard? *Yell at the kid with the ability to get the job done.*

Coach DV's criticisms were never just to make noise or vent frustration. They were frequently confusing to players and crazy-sounding to fans. They were also filled with common sense.

9.
A COMMITMENT TO UNFAIRNESS AND THE IMPORTANCE OF *REDUCING* CONFIDENCE

I played on two of Coach De Venzio's most successful teams. We went 22-5 and 25-1, and I was still never good enough to play intramurals in college. That's because I was never allowed to do anything in high school. I'm thirty-seven years old, I can't dribble; thirty-seven years old, I can't shoot. I was supposed to give it to a little guy and let him lose it, play defense, rebound, give it to someone else, stay out of the way.

— Jim Conley
Former Coach DV player
Captain of '64 Rose Bowl Champs

GET BIGSY OUT OF THERE. HE'S GOING ABSOLUTELY CRAZY. HE'S PLAYING LIKE A WILD MAN FROM BORNEO.

A Commitment to Unfairness and the Importance of *Reducing* Confidence

Have you ever wondered how many basketball players down through the years have been angry at coaches because the coaches let one kid shoot more than they let others? Multiply that number by at least two (or maybe 1.65, for the parents of those basketball players), and then add in some aunts, uncles, grandmas and grandpas, and you're getting closer to a feeling for what the typical coach hears from the peanut gallery.

So much complaining about lack of fairness, so little awareness of the facts. That was Coach DV's view. It irritated him just to think that some parents or players had any kind of gripe at all. Again, as with so many other issues, the whys and wherefores didn't usually present themselves to Coach DV, because the reality was so crystal clear to him.

"How do we know that chair is really a chair?"

This might be a great question for a college philosophy test, but for most people, the discussion isn't worth the time. There are better things, more important things to think about. The chair simply is a chair. Who really cares how we know? We just know.

Coach DV just knew—with no doubt at all—which kids should be shooting the ball and which kids should not be, and he wasn't eager to waste his time explaining.

"Coach, you let Vigrass shoot any shot he wants, but if Susa just *looks* at the basket, you're upset. It isn't fair."

Fair? Coach DV would wonder where anyone ever picked up the concept of fairness when it came to sports. Of course, it wasn't fair. How could it be fair? Why did no parent ever complain, in Coach DV's forty years of coaching, that the big strong guys got all of the rebounds and didn't leave any for the little guys?

"Holy hell, how obvious can anything get? The best rebounders get nearly all of the rebounds, the best shooters take nearly all of the shots."

"Is it true that you wouldn't let Phil and Ozzie shoot?" people used to ask Coach DV about two of the starters on his undefeated, state championship team.

"No, that's not true," Coach DV would answer. "They were both allowed to shoot anytime they got the ball within three feet of the basket and no one was around them!"

He wasn't merely being colorful. He was being logical. The kids that work all summer learning to shoot are allowed to shoot. The kids who don't work as hard and who therefore can't shoot as well are not allowed to shoot—at least not the same shots.

Any half-decent coach understands this perfectly, yet it is surprising how many coaches fumble and stutter when faced with angry parents who make accusations about "preferential" treatment.

"Hell yes," Coach DV would say. "I don't know what that big word means, but if it means that I prefer some kids to shoot and not others, then they're damn right. I like the kids to shoot who are most likely to make their shots."

It was hard for anyone to argue with that. But Coach DV didn't usually bother to make it that simple for them. He wasn't the type to calmly tell a parent to come to practice where the kid in question could be given a ball and the opportunity to shoot one hundred shots from a certain distance. Why invite the parent to practice to watch a shooting test?

Today, Coach DV might say, "That would be a good idea." But during his forty years of coaching, it never once seemed to occur to him!

What did occur to him was more like this: "How can this parent be so blind as not to realize that his son can't shoot? We don't have time to waste while one parent after another witnesses some sort of distance shooting extravaganza. The boys can play H-0-R-S-E on their own time, not on mine. I don't have time to stage horse games so dumb-ass parents can realize how bad their sons are."

This concept extended to nearly every facet of the game. One kid would try one time to dribble to the basket, and he would lose it out of bounds. Bingo! Coach DV sent a replacement to the scorer's table.

"Get Bigsy out of there," he'd say. "He's going absolutely crazy. He's playing like a wild man from Borneo."

Bigsy's parent could get very peeved after overhearing a statement like that. Gawd, he could hate Coach DV. How dare DV call his kid a wild man and yank him after one mistake.

"You let Petruny dribble all over the place," they'd say, "but my son tries one time to dribble in—and he even got fouled (but they didn't call it)—and the ball went out of bounds, and you yanked him. Don't you know what that does to a kid's confidence?"

Fans can get belligerent quickly.

"DV shoots down a kid's confidence," said another parent. "He makes 'em nervous in there the way he yells at 'em, it's a wonder they can do anything right. If he'd just let 'em play."

No one ever got a whole paragraph like that out within earshot of DV. He would have told them they were nuts before they got through the first line.

"Petruny's allowed to dribble because he's a dribbler!" he might say. "He's the best dribbler on the team. So if there are going to be any dribbling mistakes, Petruny will make them. Of course he may make two or three mistakes a game, but he dribbles all the time. If your son dribbled all the time, he'd have dozens of errors. Your son is not a dribbler. He's a nice boy. He has it rough having you for a father, but he's not a dribbler."

You can see why it was better that Coach DV didn't engage in many discussions with parents. He always said he would have been a great coach at an orphanage. He could get along with players with no trouble, but the parents? He had to say what he was thinking, and what he was thinking never went over too well with parents.

What about a bad pass? Of course, a kid could get yanked for one bad pass.

"But Ferguson just threw two bad passes! Why didn't you take *him* out?"

Again, in Coach DV's mind, it was because Ferguson was a passer. Derlink was not a passer. Derlink was just supposed to get rebounds and give the ball to somebody, not try to make any excellent or scoring passes. It was too likely he would throw the ball away. The good passes, therefore, would only be tried by the best passers. If a few passes were thrown away by the best passer, Coach DV could live with that. But he couldn't live with even one bad pass by a player whose passing percentage was ultimately much lower.

A good coach, regardless of how he explains it to parents and players, cannot embrace fairness at all when it means that each player is allowed to do the same things. Many coaches tell their players, "You're all fine shooters. If you get an open shot, shoot it."

Coach DV would have found an instruction like that ridiculous, even though he would understand that those coaches are perhaps just trying to instill confidence in their players.

"The trouble with instilling confidence in players," Coach DV would say, "is that then they will have enough confidence to shoot, and we don't want our poor shooters to feel confident! We don't want our poor shooters shooting. People claim you need balanced scoring, but you don't. You need all of your players to just do what they are good at, and leave the other things to the others."

"But my son is nervous when he gets in there; you make him afraid to shoot."

"Your son *should* be afraid to shoot. *I am afraid* when your son shoots!"

Parents were free to get as furious as they wanted to. But the rules, if "unfair," were nevertheless consistent. The best dribbler did nearly all of the dribbling; the big guys stayed near the basket for rebounds; the best shooters took nearly all of the shots.

And what about the confidence?

"You don't get confidence verbally," Coach DV was quick to say. "You get it by practicing. When your son practices enough to make himself a great shooter, he won't have to worry about being nervous, because he will be hearing me say 'Shoot!' and 'Get ready to shoot!' and then—hey, maybe you're right—he'll be confident!"

But Coach DV didn't take time to explain these concepts to parents so they could understand and maybe quit mumbling in the stands.

According to Coach DV, "What's the use? I've never met a parent yet who didn't think his son was better than he really was. What's the use of trying to explain anything to them? I'll just get mad when I realize how distorted their view is."

As a result, Coach DV developed a style that worked pretty well for him throughout his successful career.

"You can feel free to talk to me about anything you want," Coach DV would tell parents during the season, "as long as you don't mention basketball!"

That cut a lot of potential conversations short and allowed most others to remain uninitiated, which was precisely the way Coach DV preferred them!

10.
FOCUS AND LEARNING FROM VICTORIES

The most important thing I took away from the experience of playing for Dad was the feeling of overachieving, of having accomplished more than we really should have. For instance, my senior year, we never should have been 16-5. His teams always seemed to overachieve.

— Huck DeVenzio
Son of Coach DV and former Coach DV player

HE WAS LIVID, RED HOT, ANGRY, UNTOUCHABLE. NO ONE SAID A WORD TO HIM. IF THEY DID, THE WORDS WOULD BOUNCE OFF AS THOUGH THERE WAS A GLASS-STEEL-AND-TRAMPOLINE BUBBLE AROUND HIM.

Focus and Learning from Victories

The fans would be booing. The kid would have a look of gross injustice on his face. There was simply *no way* the kid stepped on the line. The whistle never should have been blown.

"The refs blew it! The refs lost the game!" That's what the fans said, and that's what the players said until the next day in practice.

Coach DV never yelled at players after a tough loss. He congratulated them for trying hard. His teams always tried hard.

"Hell, yeah they missed that last call. Galcik never stepped on that line. But Galcik gave them a chance to blow the last call by going *near* the line . . . Don't go near lines. Stay the hell away from lines . . . If you want to win, boys, you can't give the referees a chance to blow a call at the end . . . We already know they are blind . . . You can't give them a chance to call something . . . We gave them a chance to get involved and there was *no reason* to let them get involved . . . You should have stayed five feet away from that line and then there never would have been any question."

He kept his players focused entirely on what *they* had to do to be successful. The part everyone else played in the events, including referees, was almost of no concern. You might say that Coach DV was a grand believer in Murphy's Law, "If something can go wrong, it will." but with his own twist:

"If you let something go wrong, it will. But there's no reason to let anything go wrong. You don't have to go near lines. You don't have to let referees get involved. You can keep them out of the game if you just play right and do what you're supposed to do."

To Coach DV's way of thinking, even referees paid to cheat

won't call something wrong out in the open. They'll wait for some kind of hazy action where they can get away with making their call. Coach DV's teams, if they were doing what he told them to do, were supposed to stay out of hazy places.

Would an opposing player draw a foul in the last few seconds on one of Coach DV's players? Listen to one of his famous end-of-game timeout instructions.

"Okay, now listen, we're ahead; we are ahead by 4. That means we can't lose now unless we do something crazy. So don't foul them. Do you got that? *Don't foul.* Don't foul them. Let them shoot. Don't foul. Don't even go near them. Don't even look like you want to foul them. Get the hell out of the way."

Want to see a victorious coach livid after a win?

Once after that timeout, after those precise instructions, the other team threw the ball inbounds. A kid took a couple of dribbles and heaved a long one from half court. One of DV's players, nearby, waved a hand in the shooter's direction. The shot fell short. The game was over. Fans began to walk toward Coach DV to congratulate him on the big win, but he saw no one.

He was livid, red hot, angry, untouchable. No one said a word to him. If they did, the words would bounce off as though there was a glass-steel-and-trampoline bubble around him. It was almost as if any words thrown in his direction turned to daggers and sprang back at those around him. Actually, it was more like they bounced off that bubble at random and went spear-like toward anyone in the vicinity. People backed away. Coach DV, when livid, got the room. He got space even from unaware people who never saw him before. In show biz, they call that stage presence or force. On a basketball court, it's just called, "Coach DV is pissed. *Big pissed!*"

That was Coach DV's favorite time to light into his team. They could hear him coming before he got to the locker room door. The team was quiet, aware that something was up. Something had pissed off Coach DV. Most of the players would have no idea what it was, but they knew it was a matter of great importance, at least to Coach.

At the most, it would take one quick command: "Sit down!" But on the rare occasions that one quick command wasn't sufficient, a tiny extra noise from the team could incite a tirade. When Coach DV was angry and wanted to make a point, the whole world had to stand still. Not one kid could move a muscle. No manager or scorekeeper dared open a book or pick up a towel. No well-wishing fans dared making noise of any kind outside the locker room door. Coach DV demanded silence, and as he fumed, his anger grew and multiplied during the seconds he might have to wait for some outside disturbance to be quickly quelled by a knowing assistant coach. Typically, an assistant coach like Jack Heimbuecher (who worked with DV for some twenty years) would stop a disturbance with not much more than a harsh look. The people around would usually know what that meant: Coach DV was pissed.

When all was still, Coach DV might pace for a couple of seconds before beginning. "*Gawt-darn-it*, I can't believe it!" he would blurt out suddenly. Then he would pace some more, seemingly replenishing the supply of anger that may have escaped during that brief opening spurt. "Can *you* believe it, Jack?" he'd say, turning to his assistant but not really wanting an answer. "Hell no, he can't believe it. *No one could believe this*. What the hell—you guys are so *gawt*-darn dumb. *Ohhhh . . . Ahhhh!*"

He would make a noise, the kind you would expect if someone reached under a pillow to turn back some sheets and instead found a group of writhing snakes and lizards attached to his hands! It was emotion of a kind you rarely, if ever, saw in anyone. Commentators and newspaper reporters might call it "intensity" but that would hardly do it justice.

After that extended "snake-terror" noise of thorough anguish, disgust, and exasperation, Coach DV would get quiet, still obviously seething.

By the way, most of the players—maybe all—had no idea what was bothering Coach. But each feared that *he* might be the object of Coach's wrath during all of this angry turmoil.

"Bigsy, what the hell were you doing?" he might say. "Did you *try* to lose the game?"

Try to lose it? Just moments before, Bigsy had probably run off the court with his finest feeling of satisfaction that season. He had grabbed 10 rebounds, scored 14 points, and even blocked

2 shots. His parents were outside the locker room or lingering in the gym, exchanging congratulations with other parents. It was, it *had been*, Bigsy's finest hour!

But not now.

Bigsy had waved in the direction of that shooter making the desperation heave at the buzzer. Coach DV's team had won a very hard-fought victory over a good team—by 4 points. Four points!

"Four points." Coach DV would start in again, rather quiet at first. "Four points, Bigsy. Do you understand? Four points. Do you have any idea . . . *The only way* a team behind by 4 points can win a game with only two seconds left?" Coach DV returned quickly to a fever pitch, and his voice echoed down the hallways outside the locker room. Fans listened and moved closer to the door, curious to know what Coach was pissed about.

"Do you *know* how a team can gain four points in two seconds, Bigsy?"

Bigsy would nod. He did know. He distinctly remembered the timeout. He remembered Coach DV's exact words: "Don't foul. Get out of the way. *Let* them shoot." And he had done that, hadn't he? He hadn't fouled. All he had done was wave a hand toward the shooter. After all, Coach usually wanted a hand in the shooter's face. Coach emphasized, in fact, that you *never* let a shooter just shoot. You get a hand in his face. You try to distract a shooter. But Bigsy wasn't offering these or any other arguments.

"Do you know how a team can gain four points in two seconds when they have the ball behind mid-court, Bigsy? There is only one way: by making contact with a big, fat, dumb, clumsy oaf just standing there, too *gawt*-darn dumb to know enough to get his slow, fat ass the hell out of the *gawt*-darn way."

Each word was emphasized, pronounced fully and fitfully, in a way that would have pleased an English teacher working on diction and pronunciation. The words weren't slurred in the slightest. Each one came out like a fist pounding on a table.

Suddenly, with everything said, Coach DV would have a dramatic change of mood and tone. "Look, boys, I don't like hollering at you. You played a great game tonight. I'm proud of you. That was a good win. Hell, it was a great win. But think of how terrible we would all feel right now if we had fouled that last shot and the ball had somehow gone in the basket. We'd be sick. We'd all be crying. The fans outside, instead of celebrating, would all think we didn't know a thing about sports. They would wonder—and they'd be right—if I didn't bother to teach you anything and if we didn't realize that all we had to do was get the hell out of the way.

"You see, Bigsy, I don't like having to yell at you. You played your best game of the season tonight. I'm proud of you. Really I am. You grabbed some rebounds and sometimes you even looked like a basketball player out there . . ."

Whew! The pressure was off now. The tone had changed. The locker room could relax (not move yet, just relax!). Coach had essentially finished; his anger had lifted.

"But you can't wave at a player like that," Coach DV would go on. "You can't give the referee any excuse whatever to get involved and turn a celebration into a tragedy."

Coach DV would stare down at the scorebook in his hands for a moment, and then his focus would shift entirely. "But you did it, boys. You got this one. You played a good game. Okay. Let's all get showered and enjoy it. Good job."

The locker room would be free to celebrate then. Noise would get gradually louder. The door would be opened so reporters and parents and well-wishers could walk in. Coach would say a few more words to his assistant and then graciously answer reporters' questions as though he had not just totally blown up. He was as quick to forget as he was quick to correct.

If the reporters asked him about the incident that had set him off, he would downplay it. It was in the distant past, a thing that happens. But it was taken care of. Fully emphasized and now mostly forgotten.

If pressed, though, he would be happy to respond. "When you're ahead at the end, you don't want to do anything crazy that can possibly give the other team a chance to get back in the game. I thought our big boy got too close to their shooter at the end. When he waved a hand toward the shooter, he probably got within three or four feet of him. He shouldn't have been anywhere near him. He should be *twenty* feet away at a time like that. There was no reason to be even near that shooter."

He would be quick then to tell the reporters what a fine game Bigsy had played, and they would wonder what really happened. What was he keeping from them? He couldn't possibly have gotten that angry over a kid getting—by his own admission—"three or four feet away" from that shooter.

But that was precisely the kind of thing he would get angry about. He knew things that the reporters didn't. He knew things that Bigsy and his parents and the fans didn't know either.

For example, in this scenario, Coach DV knew that Bigsy might very well have fouled the shooter if that shooter had been a cleverer player who knew how to play basketball. The shooter that Bigsy had missed by four feet hadn't really thought of drawing a foul. He was just trying to get three more points for himself in the post-game box score. But what if the player had been a bit faster and stronger, a real winner, the kind of kid who looked for an edge and would try to suck a big, clumsy kid like Bigsy into fouling him? What if they had been playing against a Joe Petruny, the little point guard who had handled the ball for Coach DV for three years, who knew how to *think* the game? Petruny would easily have been able to get Bigsy to foul him. What no one but Coach DV really understood was that Bigsy had been *willing* to get in the way and willing to foul; he just hadn't had the opportunity. The opposing player hadn't given him the opportunity to make the mistake he was willing to make.

This was another cornerstone of Coach DV's insight into basketball. Most players are very willing to make mistakes, but you have to give them the *opportunity* to make the mistakes they are willing to make. It gets to sound almost like double talk, but it made perfect sense to Coach DV.

If you fail to apply pressure to a poor ball handling team, they are not going to make all the turnovers they are willing to make. If you fail to play at a feverish pace, the other team is not going to get the opportunity to show they are in poor physical condition.

There were dozens of obvious points like that. Coach DV understood them all in the moment, and they guided every move he made. If fans and players went home thinking he was crazy for the way he yelled at his team after a victory and the way he chewed out a kid who hadn't gotten within four feet of fouling at the end, so be it. They didn't understand the game the way he understood it. They didn't understand the true meaning of excellence and consistency.

They didn't even understand the wisdom of Coach DV's habit of blowing up after victories and remaining calm after defeats. Since Coach DV's teams won so often, the typical fan merely noticed that he seemed always to be pissed off, even after impressive victories. They just assumed that he must be *really* pissed off after losses.

But it didn't work that way. After losses, he was quietly supportive and philosophical. "You can't win 'em all," he'd say. "You tried hard. We'll go back to work, and we'll get 'em next time."

It was after his frequent wins that Coach DV really did his best teaching. What were the chances that Bigsy would be sucked into fouling a clever player like Joe Petruny at the end of some future big game? The chances weren't very good! Like it or not, Bigsy had learned a lesson he would probably never forget on the night of the best game of his career.

Couldn't Coach have waited? Couldn't he have just congratulated Bigsy for a great game and told him quietly, maybe the next day before practice, about "the play" at the end of the game? Perhaps, but is there anyone who believes the lesson would have sunk in as well as it did immediately after the moment?

Draw your own conclusion. Coach DV would never have considered waiting, and it would have been impossible for him to tone down his outburst. In fact, it seemed more likely that, in scenarios like this, he had used every power he possessed to keep the control he had exercised. Otherwise, everyone would witness the true meaning of the phrase "going through the roof." If Coach DV hadn't reacted when he did, the way he did, he would have been the only one that night who left the building feeling like his team had won "by luck," a game that had been in their pocket. He wanted them to know.

Hell yes, he would have been angry. Bigsy had been willing to foul.

"Ohhhh . . . Ahhhh!" That snake-terror noise. Coach DV could feel it now and then, on the way home, when everyone else was celebrating the victory.

11.
PRINCIPLES AND EXCUSES

Coach Chuck DeVenzio, a fiery as well as likable boss, doesn't believe in excuses . . .

— Bob Churovia
Sportswriter

TIRED? OH HELL, EVERYONE'S TIRED. I'M TIRED, MY GRANDMOTHER'S TIRED. RIP VAN WINKLE IS TIRED. EVERYONE'S TIRED.

Principles and Excuses

Robert Hepler, a graduate of Duke University and Harvard Law School, played both baseball and basketball for Coach DV. Hepler's father and Coach DV were longtime friends, and Hepler was my best friend in the world.

Nevertheless, Hepler decided to take a weekend trip to Dartmouth University as a football recruit in the middle of basketball season during his senior year in high school. Coach DV said no way. If Hepler wanted to go on the trip, fine, Coach understood, but he couldn't take the trip and miss basketball practice and expect to remain on the team.

Hepler, in a sense, called Coach DV's bluff. Surely the friendship between Hepler's father and Coach DV, if not the friendship between the two sons, would enable Hepler to get reinstated when he came back.

But no. Hepler was dropped from the team. Coach DV always admired Hepler and liked him, and they remain close friends to this day. But Coach DV never considered keeping Hepler on the basketball team that year. Never even considered it.

Hepler's father quit speaking to Coach DV, and a twenty year friendship came to an end. But DV never wavered from his principles. Never even considered it.

Years later, the same Robert Hepler, having graduated from Harvard Law School and being very successful in the business world, was watching one of Coach DV's teams practice over the Christmas holidays.

Oblivious to onlookers, Coach DV was barking out commands and making his non-stop exasperation clear as ever when mistakes were made on the basketball court.

"How could you not be there?" DV was yelling at a kid who had permitted a lay-up during a practice scrimmage. "How could you possibly not be there? You were there, on the side.

The shot went up, *he* ran, and you just stood there. How could you possibly just stand there?"

In typical fashion, the longer Coach DV searched for an explanation, the more livid he became. "He runs, you run. He runs, you run. What can possibly be so difficult about that? What the hell were you doing when he ran down the court? That's not Jesse Owens. That's Zurisko."

In a lower voice, showing sudden, real concern, DV would turn to Zurisko. "I'm not trying to make fun of you, Damien. You ran well that time—you did." Then Coach got loud again and his attention returned to the other kid. "But you can't let Damien Zurisko look like Jesse Owens. You have to move when he moves. You can't just stand there. This is basketball, you poor simp, basketball. Oh my, oh my, oh my. How are we ever supposed to beat anyone when you let Zurisko look like Jesse Owens?"

"You know," Hepler said, as he looked on with a mixture of admiration and amazement, "Coach DV simply refuses to acknowledge fatigue."

Hepler was right. Coach DV could yell and scream during a four-hour practice, which wasn't unheard of in his younger days, and *not once* did it ever even occur to him that a player failed to get to a certain place because he was tired. Being tired, simply, was never a consideration.

"How could he possibly not be there?" Coach DV asked, throwing his hands in the air with annoyance as he looked to the stands, seeking an answer.

If someone offered "tired," as an assistant or two did somewhere along the line, he learned fast that "tired" was not an answer Coach DV had any interest in hearing.

"Tired? Oh hell, everyone's tired. I'm tired, my grandmother's tired. Rip Van Winkle is tired. Everyone's tired. But that's no reason to give the other team an easy basket. You stop them from getting an easy basket, then you rest. Hell, you can sleep all night. But you never—got that?—you *never* give a team an easy basket. Giving an easy basket is a mortal sin. If you're a Catholic, you go to hell for that."

No one could ever tell exactly whether Coach was serious or not when he made a statement like that. He didn't really think a Catholic would go to hell for giving up an easy basket, but he certainly wouldn't have been against letting a soul burn for a few hundred years in purgatory for that kind of failure!

"You *never* give an easy basket. You got that? You guard 'em like your life depended on it. 'Cause mine does. This is what I do. I'm a coach. But how in the hell can I call myself a coach if I let you play and you let the other team just put in easy baskets? You can't give up easy baskets. You can't."

Along with fatigue came the rest of the standard excuses: upset stomachs, headaches, blisters, doctors and dentist appointments, slipping, sliding, and thinking!

"But Coach, my stomach is upset."

"Not half as upset as I am!"

"But Coach, I have a headache."

"Yeah, tell 'em you can't play because of illness; I got sick of you."

"But Coach, I have blisters on my feet."

"You have blisters on your brain."

"But Coach, I have a dentist appointment."

"Don't have a dentist appointment. Or don't make it for a time when we have practice. You don't come late to practice for a dentist appointment. Wait a minute, have I missed something? Did someone make a new rule that says dentists can only work during basketball practices? If they did, okay then, I'm sorry. Cause everyone needs good teeth. But if they didn't make that rule, then cut the crap. You gotta decide, do you want to play this game or don't you?"

"But Coach, I slid."

"Well, don't slide."

"But Coach, I thought . . ."

"Don't think. It's a bad habit. On a basketball court, you just do. You react. You're ready every minute. You move. You gotta move."

Coach DV never had an ounce of patience with even the hint of an excuse.

"But the ball . . ."

"Both teams used the same ball."

"That gym . . ."

"We both had the same gym."

"The lighting . . ."

"Hell, you can shoot in the dark if you're a basketball player."

"The footing . . ."

"Then wear skates, *gawt*-darn-it! I never told you what you had to wear on your feet, I just told you to get the ball and give it to someone. What the hell do I care if it's slippery? It's slippery for them, too."

Coach DV never cared in the least about the conditions. Early in the morning, late at night, after a long trip—it was always possible to play good basketball.

"Coach, I think I ate too much."

"And I think you crap too much. Play ball and quit crying. Do you know how lucky you are? The Good Lord gave you some legs and arms and eyes, and you're talking about how much you ate. Hell, you should be happy you have a stomach."

When anyone said anything about any negative conditions, DV could go instantly from casual, friendly conversation to a complete, angry rage. His face would writhe in a scowl that threatened to be terminal.

"Let *them* have the excuses. Let *them* talk about the conditions. We don't care about those things. We just want to play basketball. Let the other guys talk about those things; we don't even want to *think* about them. Just cut the crap and play. If you wanna play, play. If you wanna talk, talk. If you wanna be a basketball player, you cut out all that crap and just play the game. You can't be a basketball player if you're gonna crap around. You gotta decide what you wanna do."

12.
WE'RE AHEAD!

For the better part of three decades, the name DeVenzio was synonymous with basketball excellence in Western Pennsylvania, both on and alongside the court. There were the sons, Dave at North Allegheny, Huck at Springdale, and Dick at Ambridge, who contributed much to the area's basketball lore. But above all, there was Chuck, the father, the man who weaved his coaching magic and won championships at all three schools . . . In recent years, the supply of sons has run dry, but the championships have continued.

— *Pittsburgh Press*
February 13, 1980

For a few moments, Coach DV got quiet. He let the silence just take over for awhile. He stared alternately at each player . . .

We're Ahead!

This was one of Coach DV's favorite instructions. Yes, *instructions.*

He would yell it over and over during games, and opposing fans would wonder what was wrong with him. Was he just rubbing it in? Anyone could look up at the scoreboard and see that his team was ahead. They had been ahead the whole game, from the very beginning. And they were still ahead, just after the fourth quarter began, by nine points. How could his team not know THAT? What was he so excited about?

One of Coach DV's players took a shot from behind the three-point line. It bounced off the back of the rim, and the other team controlled the rebound and slowed things down. Coach DV's team got back on defense, while DV yelled to the shooter, "We're Ahead!"

Next time with the ball, still holding a 9-point lead, Coach DV's point guard deftly dribbled the ball between two defenders while DV screamed at him, "We're Ahead!"

Coach DV's star player took a pass and slashed toward the basket. The other team's center came to meet him with a 6-foot-7-incher's hand stretched high to block the shot. But DV's star went by him, dribbled under the basket to the other side, and flipped up a shot—a reverse lay-up with english—that rolled straight through the hoop.

The fans cheered, admiringly, while Coach DV went berserk. "We're Ahead!"

Just moments later, up by 11 points, Coach DV's star doubled back hoping to catch the other team napping. He barely missed a steal but ran into the offensive player waiting to receive the ball.

"Foul!" said the referee after blowing his whistle.

"Time out, time out!" Coach DV roared furiously. He couldn't wait to get his team to the bench to begin the instruction. "We're Ahead! Did you hear that? Do you see the scoreboard? We're Ahead! Not them. *Us. We are ahead. We're ahead.*"

He looked each player in the eye and screamed their faces, one by one, until all five had heard the instruction directly. *"We . . . are . . . ahead!"*

The timeout was nearly over, and all he had said was what he had already made clear to the entire gymnasium before the timeout had even been called.

"What kind of coach *is* he?" people would ask in the stands. "What's he going so crazy about? He has an 11-point lead, and he just keeps screaming that his team is ahead. Don't you think those kids know that by now? I can't for the life of me see why anyone says *he* is such a good coach. What kind of timeout was that? All he kept doing was yelling at them, telling them that they were ahead. A good coach? Huh! He's more like some kind of nut. I'm glad my son doesn't play for him. No way would I let my son play for that madman."

Fairly typical fan reactions.

For a few moments, during the last part of that timeout, Coach DV got quiet. He let the silence just take over for awhile. He stared alternately at each player. There were just about ten seconds left for further instruction, and Coach DV knew that. He didn't really need that much more time, but he liked to save a little extra time just in case. DV looked down for just a moment, then glanced back up at the scoreboard as fans leaned toward the bench—always curious—to hear what DV would end with.

Suddenly, as if thinking of it for the first time, Coach DV looked each player in the eyes his arms encircling them all, and blurted out, "We're Ahead! Do you got that? *We are ahead!*"

Then the horn sounded and the players broke the huddle and went over to the free-throw line. The game was about to resume.

No other instruction or explanation had been given during the timeout. It was entirely feasible that *some* of his players didn't really understand the point. But the good players did, and the others were either so confused or scared that they knew not to do anything crazy. They knew to work like hell and not dare make a mistake. They knew not to try anything fancy or out of the ordinary, or their butts would be on the bench in a heartbeat. They knew if a thing was difficult to just wait and hold the ball.

Though some parents might complain when the kids got home, the instruction they received during the game was perfect.

Once a month, Coach would explain exactly what he meant in one of his fits of anger, usually in a sarcastic tone. At those times, his point wasn't really to explain so much as to add fodder to his sarcasm. It was at those times that many of his instructions were best articulated.

"*We* are ahead. *They* are behind. That means if the game were to end now, *we* would win and *they* would lose. Now, since we want to win and we want them to lose, we like the situation the way it is. So, we don't *have* to go doing crazy things. We don't *have* to take long shots. We don't *have* to take fancy shots. We don't *have* to make any spectacular plays to bring the people in the stands to their feet. We don't need even one more reverse lay up. We don't need to dribble between two people, and we don't have to throw any clever passes. We don't need any clever steals. None. All we have to do is play basketball. We just have to pass to each other and move and let the clock run out. And when it runs out, then we get to jump around and hug and kiss girls in the stands, and celebrate. And *they* will have to walk off the court with their heads down.

"*They* are behind. *They* are the ones who need to throw up long shots and shoot off-balance and dribble through five people and make spectacular things happen. *They* need to take foolish chances. *They* need to steal the ball. *They* need the miracles, not us. We just have to do the easy things. And if it's not easy, then just hold the ball and wait. That's all. You need heroics when you are behind, not when you're ahead.

"When we're ahead, we just want to play nice. That's all. Play nice. Like two little girls sitting in a sandbox. Play nice. There's no need for fighting or crapping around or going crazy. Just play nice when you're ahead, that's all."

It was one of those instructions so obvious that it seemed absolutely pointless to Coach DV to discuss the details. When you're ahead, you play nice. You play calm. You play cool. You play easy. You play simple. You play nice. (Yes, he said that often.) "Just play nice."

No doubt he could have yelled "Take your time" or some such instruction, but that was actually less essential than "We're ahead!"

A player could take his time and still shoot a long shot. *That* instruction wasn't what he wanted at all. He simply wanted the team to know that they were ahead. The rest, he thought, should have been obvious to any first grader. Ahead is where you want to be. When you're ahead, you play accordingly.

The meaning of "accordingly" was as clear to Coach DV as it would have been if his team had just taken a fortress in battle. It is easy to imagine Coach DV exhorting some troops:

"Don't go down there to fight. We fought to take this hill so *we* could be the ones with the advantage, so *we* could see them clearly and they couldn't see us. So *we* would have gravity on our side as we swing our weapons down, so *we* would have good footing, good vision, and the advantage. My gawd, you don't take a hill and then run down it to fight down there. Let *them* lose their footing, let *them* slip and fall. Let *them* try the daring, foolhardy raids. All we have to do is stand behind these stones and wait, and when they come, we just shoot them. *We* have the hill. *They* have to run up hill, aiming at air; *they* have to worry about us. We don't have to worry. We just have to sit here calmly and wait. *They* are the ones who have to do something. We don't have to do anything but sit here and relax."

Coach DV had been in enough desperate situations in his life, as any coach or athlete has, to realize the enormous difference between having to catch up at the end of a game and having a lead at the end. It literally caused him pain to watch basketball players play as though they had no awareness of the difference.

Watching a team with a lead take long shots and reverse lay-ups and then foul was truly as crazy to Coach DV as a soldier would be for leaving an impregnable position on a hill to fight in some trenches at a disadvantage. It made no sense at all.

A person just has to know when he is in the driver's seat and he has to drive accordingly.

13.
ERRORS BEGET ERRORS

Every time I go back to Pennsylvania, I run into a few of the guys and always your name comes up. You have made more friends and done more for young guys than anyone I know. I'm not trying to write a testimonial, but I assure you as God is my witness that I and many others feel the same. Knowing you has been one of the highlights of my life.

— Tom Tabacek
Former Coach DV player

COACH DV, FAR FROM BLOWING UP, WAS NODDING AS HE WALKED ACROSS THE GYM TOWARD THE LOCKER ROOM—NODDING IN ACKNOWLEDGMENT THAT HIS IDEAS ABOUT LIFE AND BASKETBALL HAD ONCE AGAIN BEEN CONFIRMED.

Errors Beget Errors

Coach DV's player had the ball. Time was running out. The opposing fans had just about given up any hope. Then all of a sudden, everything changed. The kid with the ball got knocked down, the ball trickled loose, and the home team got the ball and threw it down court. The kid who caught the ball mishandled it and took three steps (some people said four) as he moved to the basket for the lay-up that gave his team the victory.

The fans rooting for Coach DV's team were furious. Coach DV's player had clearly been knocked to the floor; then the final basket was scored by a kid who had taken four steps. No way! It just couldn't be.

"They cheated us."

"We got robbed."

"Our kid got knocked down. This ain't football."

"I'd like to kill those referees."

Even the athletic director assured the fans that those guys would never again officiate another game if he had anything to do with it.

"It was a travesty," one fan said. "The worst job of reffing I've ever seen."

But Coach DV didn't hear any of it. And what's more, he didn't agree.

Oh sure, his player had indeed been knocked to the court. He'd been literally pushed to the ground by two defenders. And the kid at the other end? He had clearly traveled with the ball. Coach DV had seen it all, but none of it mattered to him as he walked into the locker room to talk to his angry team.

"Shut up!" he shouted. Coach was not in the habit of showing anger after losses, but he had overheard a couple of players blaming the referees. "The fans can talk about it if they want, but not us. You got fouled, Riley, and that kid walked, but that shouldn't have meant crap."

Only one thing was on Coach DV's mind: what had happened on the play just before "the one that lost the game." Coach DV's team had the ball—and a 3-point lead—and the time was ticking away: 20 . . . 19 . . . 18 . . . 17 . . . Suddenly, one of Coach DV's players was called for an offensive foul when he was nowhere near the ball! It was unheard of. Not one fan had even seen it. It almost never happens, but it did that night. The other team got the ball and made a quick basket, cutting the margin to one and setting the stage for the final foul-and-walk that made the fans blow up.

But Coach DV, far from blowing up, was nodding as he walked across the gym toward the locker room—nodding in acknowledgment that his ideas about life and basketball had once again been confirmed. The fans' ideas were totally foreign to his own because there was never any concept more consistent in Coach DV's philosophy than the assurance that *errors beget errors*. When you make a mistake first, you just have to expect that someone else is going to make one, too. One, too. One, two. You make a mistake, he makes one, too. The solution was not to start the chain. Not to make the first error.

Coach DV went on with his post-game talk to his players. "There was *no reason* for them to be within one point of us. *No reason,*" he blurted for emphasis. "You don't *ever* frack with a kid away from the ball. Once you do that, you know you're going to lose. You *deserve* to lose when you do that. We can't expect the referees to be smart if we're so *gawt*-darn dumb ourselves."

Coach DV's kid had been held. A defender was grabbing his shirt and, to get away, he pushed at the kid and got called for the foul. Unlike the fans, Coach DV had seen it clearly. He had a sixth sense about looking in the right direction, about knowing what was likely to go wrong. He never seemed to miss anything of importance that happened on a basketball court.

The kid charged with the foul had a pained expression on his face, but he was smart enough not to make excuses at a time like this. Nevertheless, Coach DV saw the expression.

"I know their kid was holding your shirt," he told the kid.

"But you have to expect that at the end of a game. They were desperate. They were losing. They had to try something. You had to expect that."

Coach DV hated to dwell on a final mistake, though. He always said that games were never won in the last minute, but in the 31 minutes before. It was a natural extension of his errors-beget-errors philosophy.

"You can't crap with a guy holding your shirt at the end of a game. You can't push him away. You gotta *move*—you can't give the referees a chance to call anything. Of course they're gonna blow calls at the end. They get nervous, too. But we never should have given them the chance to blow the game. They never should have had a chance. I told you at halftime, you guys were not playing ball. You should have run this team right off the court, but you crapped around and Gary got those dumb-ass fouls . . ."

His voice trailed off for a moment. He really didn't like to criticize after a loss. He wouldn't have done it at all, except he could never let a game like that end with his players mumbling—and listening to their parents say—that the referees had lost the game.

"I don't want to holler at you, boys. You tried hard. You did. You tried hard. But this was *our* game, and we let them take it from us. The referees didn't take it from us. *We* let it get away.

Okay, that's all. We'll be okay. Let's get our showers and put it behind us."

He turned to his assistant coach. "How can we be so *gawt*-darn dumb? That could only happen to us."

Actually, it happened to teams all the time, but it didn't happen very often to Coach DV's teams. Coach DV's teams didn't lose many games by doing dumb things at the end. Not many of Coach DV's players ever punched or pushed at a guy holding their shirts. They had learned to expect such things and to ignore them routinely. They were always a lot more concerned about The Man on the Bench watching their every move than the guys on the court holding their shirts.

By the end of preseason scrimmages, Coach DV's players usually knew not to "play patty cake with some fat kid who just wants to play grabby-grabby." They knew that, especially at the end of games with a lead, they had to "play basketball," which (though seldom explained) meant cutting out all extraneous crap and sticking to the two great commandments: "Move your fat tail and move the ball!"

They knew that if they'd done that, the referees, the foul at the end, and the walk wouldn't have made a bit of difference. That was the only way to think, if you wanted to be a winner, Coach DV always said. That was the only way to win.

14.
DON'T GET FOULED!

I never thanked you for the things you taught me at North Allegheny. I didn't play basketball beyond high school. But with your help, I was able to develop character traits that I have been able to apply in my life. I developed self-confidence playing under you. You motivated me to persevere under adversity. You taught me the importance of hard work. You also told me to have "gumption" and "not to take crap off anybody." I know these aren't eloquent words, but they are your words, and they had a lot of meaning to a high school kid.

— Richard J. Gass
Former Coach DV player

HOW COULD YOU HELP IT IF A BIG GUY DECIDED TO FOUL YOU? HOW COULD A COACH BE SO DUMB NOT TO BE ABLE TO SEE THAT?

Don't Get Fouled!

Coach DV's almost-daily command not to get fouled drove me crazy for years, as it did many players. Think about it. You'd go driving into the basket during a practice scrimmage, and you'd get fouled and miss the shot. The second team would get the rebound and start down the other way, while you'd look at Coach DV expecting him to call the foul.

Why do basketball players always expect fouls to be called? It's bad enough expecting a referee to call one, but expecting a coach to acknowledge a foul is fruitless. A good coach is interested in how tough you are, how you react to adversity, how quickly you get back on defense. He cares little about fouls. That's not his department, at least not during practice.

But that wasn't really the point. A kid on Coach DV's team understood all that. Coach DV made that clear.

"Never expect anything from a referee. If you get a call someday, consider it a gift. But never expect it. Play as though they are *not* going to call anything."

You didn't expect Coach DV to actually call the foul, but you did *not* expect what he did do: *He would yell at you for getting fouled!*

It would begin with that missed shot and "the look," his seemingly ever-present scowls of disgust.

"Don't throw up that crap," he would say.

"I was fouled!"

"Well, don't get fouled."

Don't *get* fouled? What the hell did that mean? How could you help it if you got fouled? You're on your way to the basket, you're playing by the rules—you even made a pretty good play—you got by your defender, and then a big guy came over and just smacked you across the arm. What the hell could you do about that? How could you help it if a big guy decided to foul you? How could a coach be so dumb he couldn't see that?

I can't recall Coach DV ever really explaining the point. I'm not sure if he withheld it on purpose or just never thought to explain. He would always be the first one to admit: "I'm not very good at explaining things."

He wasn't very good because it was all so crystal clear to him, like everything else in the game of basketball.

So, why did he frustrate hundreds of players through the years, urging them not to get fouled? Well, if a player wanted to be good, he couldn't rely on a referee's call. But more importantly, he had to recognize that he wouldn't always be playing against the second string on his school team. The days would come soon enough, if he wanted to be good, that he would find himself in games against other stars—taller, tougher, stronger stars—and then the referee wouldn't even be a factor. Those players would be able to block shots that the second stringers in practice could only get near enough to commit fouls.

But players tend not to think in those terms. To use a common sports cliché, players tend to "take 'em one at a time," thinking mostly about the present and playing against the guys that are out there on that particular day.

On the other hand, Coach DV, and no doubt all great coaches, are always competing against champions. They are constantly aware of what it takes to be successful against real stars.

When a kid makes a mediocre move to the basket and gets fouled by an awkward sophomore, the kid just feels the foul. But a Coach DV sees players on other teams and in future games blocking those shots and dunking—and gloating—at the other end. When he said, "Don't get fouled!" that was precisely what he meant.

"If you choose to take a shot and go so slowly that one of our second stringers in practice can foul you, then a star later on—in a real game—will block that shot and make you look sick."

It was that simple. Don't get fouled. Don't make mediocre moves at all. Don't even think about them. Make moves so clever and so decisive that a defender can't even follow you with his eyes, let alone his feet. That was basketball, according to Coach

DV, and that was the way Coach DV prepared each of his players on each of his teams for forty consecutive years.

If they wondered why he never seemed satisfied, it was because he constantly measured performance against championship standards. Not many coaches—or everyday people—do that on a minute by minute, day by day basis for forty years.

15.
APPEARANCES COUNT

I'd say he is *the most dynamic coach I know . . . He is a warm gentleman at heart, but he expects you to do it his way. I've never seen him throw chairs, but I've seen him throw basketballs. He gets his point across. He's a great motivator. And now he's a great friend.*

— Coach Jack Derlink
Former Coach DV player

A guy like Henry's too dumb to know he's ugly, so he walks around like he's somebody important—and the girls believe him!

Appearances Count

Appearances were important, even crucial, to Coach DV. No, he didn't care much about uniforms; he didn't care if they were out of style, faded, too big or too small. Uniforms didn't matter.

He didn't care much about shoes, either. Are they two or three sizes too big? "That's okay, just stuff with 'em with socks; they'll be fine."

He was serious. He routinely expected people to make do.

If one day each of his players came out wearing different kinds of sneakers, he never would have noticed, though game after game his players all wore the same school-supplied shoes. He wouldn't even have noticed if they all suddenly changed from white low-cuts to orange high tops. Shoes just didn't matter.

Coats 'n' ties on the road? A team ought to look sharp when traveling, right? "If that's what the school wants, or the athletic director, fine. Does everyone have a coat 'n' tie?"

Coach DV didn't care about dressing up. He always wore a tie himself, but that was simply because teachers were expected to. For his own part, he never noticed. He only worried if everyone had whatever the school's dress code required. He remembered very well a time in his youth when he did not have those things. He went one winter in high school without a coat or even a jacket. But he didn't make an issue out of that. He wore a couple of sweaters or sweat shirts. No big thing.

"Hey, Coach, what do you want to do about Henry?" an assistant asked.

"I don't know. Did something happen to him?" Coach DV wasn't aware that there was anything to do about Henry.

"He's got that growth coming on his chin."

"Has he seen a doctor?"

Coach DV didn't make the connection. According to the assistant, over the Christmas holidays, one of the seniors was "testing the system."

"He's proud of it, Coach, and I think he's testing us."

"He's proud of what? What the hell are you talking about?" Coach DV finally asked, impatient and irritated with the assistant.

"That beard. Henry's growing a beard."

"Isn't he allowed?" Coach DV wanted to know.

"Well," the assistant said, "you know there's a school rule against it."

No, Coach DV didn't know, even though he would be quick to admit that the rule may have been in place for the preceding ten years. "I may have known it once, I don't know. But if it's a rule, then it's a rule. Tell him to cut it off."

It was no big thing. He really didn't understand why the assistant had even brought it to his attention. He never guessed that an assistant might feel intimidated by a star player. Hell, there was nothing to be intimidated about. Beards were a million miles from Coach DV's mind. If it was a rule, then the beard had to be cut off. What could be simpler?

And what's all this crap about a test? Instead of tiptoeing around the situation as the assistant had done, Coach DV just hit everything head on. He didn't care about testing any systems. He cared about winning basketball games. But, now that it had been brought to his attention as some sort of problem, Coach DV would handle the thing immediately. He always wanted "all the bullshit" out of the way.

"Henry," he said, walking out to the court before practice began. "Is there a school rule against beards?"

"Yes, Coach."

"Is that fuzz on your chin a beard?"

"I don't know, Coach."

"I don't know either. It doesn't look like much of anything to me. You look like Foo Man Choo's brother, Tobacco Chew, and you got it all over your chin! But you better find out if you're allowed to have that or not. We don't want any bullshit over something like that."

Coach DV would leave the subject completely, not aware that there was anything left to discuss. He would call the team together to start practice and concentrate entirely on basketball, on what the team needed to do better in the coming games. Then, once he felt he had a handle on things and he had established the tone for the day, his mind would come back to the beard.

"Do girls actually like that thing, Henry?" Coach DV wanted to know in all seriousness. Then he'd contort his face like he did when he was very angry during a game, and he'd say something like: "Girls must be nuts!"

He'd pause for a few moments, then look over at his assistant. "Ah, it's great to be young. A guy like Henry's too dumb to know he's ugly, so he walks around like he's somebody important—and the girls believe, him! It's great, isn't it, Henry?"

Suddenly, he's back to basketball, totally immersed in it, his face crinkling up again, only this time because he recalls one of the players who kept standing too far out during the last game, failing to get back to cover the basket when he was away from the ball playing a matchup zone.

"You gotta get *back*. You gotta get *back*. You *can't* let them in for an easy basket. You *gotta* get back. There's no one else."

The beard had been totally forgotten, and Coach hadn't felt tested in the least. Those kinds of appearances didn't make a bit of difference to Coach DV. The appearances that mattered were not clothes-related, hair-related, or rule-related. They were basketball-related, athlete-related.

"You gotta *look* like a basketball player. Don't stand there like a pregnant lady. Stand like a *bas*ketball player. Get down, get ready, like this. You see, you get down, you bend your knees, and you look ready to move. You go up, you go back. You go left, you go right. You're ready. You're always ready. I know I've told you this before, but you gotta *do* it. It doesn't do any good for me to keep talking if you're not gonna do it. You gotta do it. If you want to play this game, you gotta *look* like a player. Even an old fat man like me looks more like a basketball player than you do. You gotta get down. You gotta move—or at least be ready to move."

"Looking like a basketball player" extended to the way you

stood during a time out, the way you lined up for a jump ball, the way you waited on defense for the other team to bring the ball down the court, the way you warmed up before practice.

If you failed to do any of those things, Coach could blow up at you for the way you were standing before anything even happened.

"That's why you have to go to games or watch on TV. Watch the way good players play, and then *you* do what they do. There's no secret. I'm not telling you something I got off the pyramids in hieroglyphics. I'm just telling you what you can see any time you go to watch real basketball players. They *look* like basketball players. You can't play basketball until you look like a basketball player. You gotta watch what they do, and then just do that. Don't watch old fat men and pregnant ladies. Watch basketball players. If you want to be good, then do what good players do."

16. INJURIES AND THE ONE-SECOND DECISION

You must have many fond memories of your career as one of the most successful coaches in the history of Pennsylvania. Judy and I both have a warm spot in our hearts when we talk about you and your tremendous achievements in athletics. Our children have never met you, but they feel like they know you because of our Coach DV stories.

— Nick and Judy Pinchok
Former Coach DV students

WE DON'T WANT YOU TO DIE ON US, SON. YOU TAKE A SHOWER, AND IF YOU'RE STILL ALIVE, MAYBE YOU CAN PLAY THE NEXT GAME.

Injuries and the One-Second Decision

The business world is familiar with the "One-Minute Manager." Well, Coach DV did that concept fifty-nine better with his one-second decision!

Anyone who has watched youth basketball—in fact, basketball at just about any level—has seen the situation that brought about Coach DV's one-second decision. Regardless of where it happens, it goes something like this:

A kid gets knocked down—or trips or falls—on his offensive end of the court. The fall undoubtedly causes him to lose control of the ball, or he misses a shot having expected a foul to be called. He has messed up in some way, and he's lying on the ground "in pain." (In quotes, because it's the kind of pain that makes a mother wince, along with a handful of inexperienced fans. Everyone else knows that this is one of those quasi-injuries destined to be gone moments later.) The kid remains on the floor, perhaps grimacing or holding whatever hurts. The game goes down to the other end without him, and most everyone watches the 5-on-4 except for the kid's mother and the few fans who think the kid is really injured.

Sometimes those special loving few find themselves screaming at the referees and cussing them out for ignoring an injury. Like the kid, they are partly angry that the injury is being ignored, but they are mostly upset that his play or move was unsuccessful and—My gawd! It couldn't have been a mistake!—no foul was called.

"C'mon Ref, you blind SOB. What's it gonna take? They knocked the kid down. Blow that whistle, you jerk."

The injustice, coupled with the fall, immobilizes the kid. How badly is he injured? Is something broken? Will he miss the entire season?

Naturally, there *are* some injuries of a serious nature. But much more often—maybe 90 percent of the time—the kid makes a miraculous instant recovery the moment his team regains possession of the ball. Suddenly he is on his feet, jumping up and down and waving his arms, yelling, screaming, pleading for the ball before the other team wakes up and gets back to cover him. Glory to God! Throw down your crutches and walk! The kid is fine.

Back in the late Forties, Coach DV saw all he ever wanted to see of those plays. He didn't like the odds of 5-on-4, hated the concept of any player loafing on defense, and wasn't an avid believer in miracle cures—at least not those that occurred on basketball courts.

"We don't have miracle cures here," Coach DV would tell his teams. "We don't want players lying on the court. In West Virginia they shoot guys like that to put them out of their misery! We don't have time for you to nurse an injury and get attention from the fans for something that's gonna be better a few moments later. If you want attention on this team, you get it by playing basketball, not by nursing injuries."

With that, he made it very simple.

"If you get injured, jump up and play—*within one second*—or plan on calling it a day. We'll bring out a stretcher and we'll get you to the hospital. No use you staying on the court. If you're hurt, you need to be someplace where someone can help you. And if you're not hurt, then jump up and play. It's up to you. You decide. Just decide quickly. Because we don't want to lose a basket while you decide whether or not you're hurt."

The easy way, Coach DV always explained, was just to assume you weren't hurt. Assume the pain will be leaving, and just go on as though nothing had happened.

"If there's a bone sticking out of your leg when you try to jump up, obviously you won't jump too well, and we'll all understand. No one expects you to play with a bone sticking out of your skin, and you won't want to play either. So, in that case, it will be fine with everyone if you just hop off the court! If you're really hurt, there won't be any problem. But if you're not, we don't have time to frack with you. A little pain is good for you every once in awhile."

With The Rule in place, a kid had to make a quick decision. That little bit of extra attention for a fall would be very costly. If he wasn't really hurt, he'd find himself on the way to the showers, although he felt fine before he even turned on the water.

"Get a shower," Coach DV would say.

But a young player might object. He may not have heard about this rule. Coach DV's rules weren't written down and handed to players in a notebook at the beginning of each season; they were sort of passed down, from year to year, or from generation to generation. Or players learned them the hard way, straight from the horse's mouth through gruff corrections. "DV has no patience with injuries," they would say. Young players were just supposed to know these things or else learn fast.

"I'm okay, Coach. I can play."

"No you can't."

"I feel fine, Coach. I'm okay."

"No, you're hurt, son. We all saw you."

The sarcastic tone might take over to emphasize the point because often a young player would just think Coach DV had misunderstood him.

"I'm okay, Coach. I can stay in."

"No, son, you're hurt. We know you're hurt because you lay there on the floor like a dead man while just four of your teammates had to guard five. No one who is okay would ever do that. Hell, I've seen folks down at Barney Clowe's [the local funeral home] look better than you did out there. We don't want you to die on us, son. You take a shower, and if you're still alive, maybe you can play the next game."

It took only one of those per season for the message to sweep across the team. "DV doesn't like injuries. You either jump up and play immediately or go to the showers."

Coach DV allowed no gray areas when it came to injuries and sickness. Either you were real sick or really injured—in which case, everyone could sincerely sympathize with you—or you weren't sick or injured at all.

Don't talk to Coach DV about sore feet and jammed fingers

and headaches and colds. "Don't be a grandmother," he'd say. "Make a decision. Do you want to play or don't you? If you want to play, then play. If you're sick, you're sick."

There were no in-betweens.

17.
BUILDING CONFIDENCE:
OFFHANDED COMMENTS, *SCORE!* AND THE GOOD LORD

To this day, I am amazed how you seemed to sense how to get the most out of each of us. Some responded only when you punctuated your point with an airborne basketball, while others like myself responded when you explained what went wrong and offered an approach to correct the mistake . . .

— Bob C. Anderson
Former Coach DV player

The huddle would break and Coach DV was all smiles. He wasn't tense at all. The shots would go up, just like he said, and they would drop right in.

Building Confidence: Offhanded Comments, *Score!* and the Good Lord

Though Coach DV was often criticized for tearing down athletes' confidence, he was actually a master at building it.

The criticism came nearly always in the same form: some parents were upset because their son was afraid to shoot or afraid to take initiative since Coach DV would take him out of the game for one bad pass or one missed shot.

In a sense, the parents were correct. Coach DV would be quick to inform them that he didn't want their son to be confident, that their son wasn't good enough yet to try things or to take shots, so if their son did overstep his ability level, he deserved to come out! What could be simpler? In their son's case, DV wasn't interested in building confidence. Their son had to build his own confidence by significantly increasing his skill level.

On the other hand, Coach DV's methods for inspiring confidence in his good players were very effective. At times they were very subtle; at other times, very direct. Regardless of what methods or words Coach DV used, they always had real impact because they were backed with such conviction.

It wasn't so much "You can do it!" as it was "What the hell is wrong with you? You *know* you can do *that!*"

Many times, the athlete may not have known he could do the particular thing Coach DV was talking about, but he certainly believed he could once Coach had dismissed any other notion as pure horse manure.

When a star wasn't performing up to par, Coach DV didn't tiptoe around his feelings.

"You're the All-American, Denny, not *him*. Now *gawt*-darn-it, cut out all the shit and play ball. We don't have time to crap around with little kids out there. If you keep playing like this, you'll get them thinking they *are* good, and then we *will* have trouble. Shit. That kid couldn't stay with my mother. Gawt-darn-it, *play ball*."

On paper, his words may not appear particularly inspiring, but those words, delivered with his angry intensity, registered with every player who ever played for Coach DV.

Sometimes, the methods would be very different. Instead of yelling at his star, Coach DV would be uncharacteristically quiet. At least at first.

"Denny, are you sick?" he would ask, from all appearances showing total concern and sincere curiosity. "No? Did something happen to you today at school?" once again asked with the same quiet, sincere manner. "No? Is something wrong at home? Did something happen to someone in your family?"

The star would be shaking his head. No, no, no, nothing was wrong.

Coach DV might try one more question, and any veteran player would know that the tension, despite the outward calm, was mounting, earthquake-like. "Did some girl do something to you?"

No again.

Coach DV could hardly take it any longer. "Am I missing something? I'm serious. Is there something you can't talk about? Please, tell me. I won't ask for details. I'll let you alone. I just want to know."

"No, Coach," the star would finally say, "I'm just not playing well."

Blowup!

"You're telling *me* you're not playing well! You're not doing a *gawt*-darn thing. You're runnin' like your feet are in quicksand, and you're rebounding like you're a *gawt*-darn little sissy. Are you afraid of someone out there?"

"No."

"Well, *gawt-darn-it!* What the hell are you doing? You're playing like a kid who never saw a ball before. You're embarrassing me and your parents and your friends. If *that* doesn't matter to you, don't you have any pride in yourself? You should be ashamed to walk in here and say nothing's wrong. What the hell you mean, nothing's wrong? Everything is wrong. You practice all summer and you're playing like a guy who never touched a ball. Hell, I could understand it if you just did this as a hobby. But this is *your* sport. This is your bread and butter. It's like they're taking food right off your table, and you don't have the *gawt-darn guts* to do anything about it. *Ohhhh* shit, I never thought I'd have to talk this way to *you*. Denny, you put too much time into this game to play like this. You can't play like this, boy. I don't know what you're hiding. I don't give a shit if you are sick. You can't play like this. *Play ball!*"

Invariably, after a "talk" like that, the star would come out in the second half, *smoking*!

Offhanded Reassurance

Perhaps Coach DV's most outstanding method of conveying belief to a player (it was *very* effective) occurred during timeouts, late in close games, when the pressure was really on—something like one point behind with a couple of free throws to shoot.

A player about to shoot pivotal free throws can get extremely nervous anticipating his task. Make both free throws, and everyone would be cheering and screaming and calling him the hero. But miss both, and the whole crowd would be groaning. Everyone would know that he blew it under pressure, that he "lost the game." Car after car would be driving home shortly after, each passenger unable to help reiterating what would have happened had those free throws been made.

Regardless of the specific thoughts any individual player may have, all players think essentially the same thing: Will I be the hero or the goat? Will there be celebrations or tears? There isn't much middle ground when games are on the line.

Often, opposing coaches call timeouts before big pressure shots just so the shooter has more time to think and anguish over the importance of what he is about to do.

Many coaches have difficulty containing their own nervousness at these times. In recent years, television has shown some of the nation's best-known coaches hiding their eyes or looking away because they can't bear to watch those crucial final shots.

But Coach DV was the other side of the coin. The tension, the anger, the hawk-like determination normally visible during every practice, every halftime, and during nearly every play, would suddenly get replaced. Coach would get a big smile on his face. He would become completely relaxed. He would thoroughly enjoy the moment.

"This," he would say, "is what it's all about, boys. This is why you play basketball. Look at all those fans, all so concerned about this game. Let's enjoy this. Isn't this fun now, boys? This is fun."

My brother calls Coach DV "Mr. Equilibrium." When everyone else seems calm, he is angry, screaming, demanding, creating tension. But when others are nervous, he is the picture of tranquility and relaxation.

In these final seconds, during the timeout, just before the crucial free throws, Coach DV would spend his time on other things. He would turn to his best rebounder and talk to him about getting the rebound and going up strong for the winning basket. If behind in the score, he would talk about defense in the last few seconds. But mostly he would talk about how to play (assuming his team would be ahead).

Far from pleading with the free throw shooter to make these free throws, he ignored the free throw shooter and concentrated on everyone else. Only, it would seem, as an afterthought would he mention that it wasn't very critical whether or not the shots were made.

"Vernon always hits well under pressure, but it doesn't matter," he would say. "If he happens to miss one, you guys just have to play ball and get the rebound. You can't expect Vernon to do everything."

He might turn to his assistant, being sure that everyone and especially Vernon, the nervous shooter, could hear him. "I'm not worried about Vernon. Of course he's nervous. He'd be crazy not to be. But it doesn't depend on Vernon. We know Vernon will put up a soft shot and follow through and give the ball a great chance to go in. But if the ball happens not to go in, there's nothing Vernon can do about it. If we want to win, we have to get the rebound. That's all there is to it. We can't expect Vernon to win every game for us. If he makes them, fine; then he's the hero at the dance. But if he happens to miss one, there's no reason one of the other guys can't be a hero. Big Shoe, you have anything against being the hero?"

"No, Coach."

"Then let's get that ball and put it in the basket!"

The huddle would break and Coach DV was all smiles. He wasn't tense at all. The shots would go up, just like he said, and they would drop right in some days, and on other days they would miss. Should the shots not fall, he really wouldn't blame Vernon. Vernon had gotten that message loud and clear. Coach DV just thought it was nice for Vernon to have the opportunity to be a hero. If he missed, hey, you can't make 'em all. No one makes 'em all.

Nobody walked out to the lane pleading with Vernon either. They had their assignments: Don't line up hoping Vernon does it. Get yourself in position to get the rebound and win it when he misses. Coach DV would emphasize: "We ain't walking up there *hoping*; we're walking up there *doing*."

This made a world of difference in the attitude of every player. In that brief timeout talk, Coach DV had made it clear that there was no blaming Vernon if he failed to make the free throws. It was still everyone's chance to be a hero, if Vernon missed. Vernon felt that pressure lifted at the same time, and he felt confident. He had never known that Coach DV had that kind of confidence in him. Coach DV's words rang in his ears. "Vernon always hits well under pressure. Vernon will put up a soft shot and follow through."

There weren't any instructions. No tension. Just an offhanded reminder and an offhanded compliment. Psychologically, he put every player in a frame of mind to be successful, and he took the pressure off the guy who was supposed to have it all.

In forty years of coaching, very few of Coach DV's players ever missed crucial end-of-game free throws, and when they did, none of them ever felt like they'd lost the game. The team lost it. On the other hand, many players stepped up to that line in crucial situations and felt free to grasp the heroics. Guys like

Curt Carson who, with no time left on the clock and one point behind in the state championship, with the home fans shaking the board and rim, calmly sank two free throws and handed their rival their only loss of the year.

There was no one better than Coach DV at instilling confidence when it really counted.

Score!

Another of Coach DV's favorite, confidence-inspiring tactics was even simpler, yet equally effective—no doubt because he had the knowledge and feel for the game to enable him to know exactly when his order could best be carried out.

What was this awesome, subtle, clever tactic?

Coach DV, in his inimitable, aggressive style, would grab his star by the shirt and scream one word from the depths of his stomach; or if the play were actually going on, he would stare at his star, shake a fist at him, and scream the same word: *"Score!"*

Score? "Is that all?" an unknowing fan might ask. Probably only another great basketball coach or great leaders in other walks of life would really understand.

"Score!" wasn't a hope that could be yelled to the team every time down the court. It was a command issued to a star at a time when Coach DV perceived that the conditions were just right to cut out all the bullshit, drop all the confusion, forget about methodology, and just *inject your ability authoritatively into the fray right now*. No ifs, ands, or buts. Just do it. Put the ball in the basket. Use your best play, your power move or your slashing drive, but do it now—right now—no more questions. *Score!*

Fans sitting near the bench, seeing how effective the order was, wondered why he didn't just yell it all the time. But of course Coach DV knew. Sports people knew. There are things that great coaches see that the rest of us don't notice. There are times to act. Times to depart from the script. Times to just do it. Coach DV was a master at picking those times.

When he told a kid to score, it was like handing him a free pass, a plaque, some magic shoes, some super-human speed and strength, and a lifetime of validation. The order told the kid everything, all in the one elongated, nearly blood curdling edict: SCORE!

That one word meant: "I have confidence in you; you have worked hard; you are a good player; you are better than the guy guarding you; he can't stop you and neither can his team; the time is right for you to just do your thing; don't worry one bit about the outcome. I'll take the blame if you miss; just go in there with power and pride and show them what the hell you are made of because I know what you're made of. *You are the best.*"

What a validation coming from a coach who is always pissed, always unsatisfied, always uneasy, usually disgusted. When Coach DV picked spots to tell his stars to score, they scored.

The Good Lord

Coach DV could impart the same kind of confidence to his whole team. He had a saying he used often. It wasn't really as much of a religious statement as it may seem. Mostly, it was just a way to explain simply an unexplainable phenomenon.

"You see, you do things right, and the good lord puts it in for you. Move your fat tail, move the ball, and it's like magic! You'll find yourself open and the shot will go in."

"I don't know if the good lord really puts the ball in," DV would say. "I can't really think the lord watches high school basketball games or cares which team wins, but the world just seems to be set up that way, if you want to really know the truth. If you move the ball and move your tail, in a short time, someone gets open; and he can tell, as the ball swings to him, that he's going to have the shot; and it's going to be a good shot, and it's a shot everyone will agree with; and he'll have time to get set and on balance; and—dammit—I don't know why, but those shots just seem to go in a helluva lot more often than when a team craps around and has to throw the ball at the basket.

"There may be no lord or magic in that at all. But when you see it work as long as I have, you have a certain feeling about it. I don't know what to call it. I just always said, 'if you do things right, the good lord will put it in for you,' because there's really no way to explain it. It's not really that you make 'em all, but you make so many more, and you even seem to get so many more rebounds if you do miss . . . the guys are in the right places, the defense has had to scramble to keep up, so they aren't ready and you are . . . I'm sure Dean Smith and John Wooden have statistics on why this works. Personally, I never really cared. I just knew that it worked."

If you do things right, the good lord will put it in for you.

"You play like crap, you don't deserve to score. You see, the good lord's not going to reward you when you crap around. You don't have to believe in the lord to see that. You can't crap around in this game. You just can't crap around."

Like golfers getting into a groove, Coach DV's teams—after all that yelling and screaming in practice, after all the constant repetition, and amidst consistent exasperation—would usually jell in games.

It was a thing of beauty. Short, snappy passes, bodies moving swiftly. They didn't have the talent of college or pro teams, but they typically ran their plays much better. They moved. And they moved the ball. Even though the opposing coaches knew exactly what they were going to do, the plays kept working and working, despite his using the *same* plays for over thirty years.

They worked because of the swiftness and precision of the execution. It didn't matter that the other team knew what they were going to do, they didn't have any way to stop it. Tungo, tungo, tungo. Three quick passes, three quick cuts, and *bingo!*—the good lord put it in.

"You see, when you do it right, you can kick it up there and it will go in. You just gotta play *bas*ketball."

18.
THE PERFECTIONIST PHILOSOPHY:
INSURMOUNTABLE LEADS, EARLY CELEBRATIONS, AND THE HALFTIME TALK

Happiness is going to one of the PDS basketball games. I always mark the games on my calendar. As far as I am concerned, we have a regal team. Our players give 100 percent all of the time, and they always hustle. Mr. DeVenzio deserves a medal for coaching. I bet all the other teams are jealous of him. I am proud to have him representing our school.

— Wes Robinson
7th grader (at the time of writing)

LEADS ARE OFTEN TEMPORARY, MOMENTUM SHIFTS, SPORTS ARE FICKLE, AND THE DIFFERENCE BETWEEN VICTORY AND DEFEAT IS SO OFTEN AN INCREDIBLY THIN LINE.

The Perfectionist Philosophy:
Insurmountable Leads, Early Celebrations, and the Halftime Talk

What is a real perfectionist? What does this concept look like in action, in real life—on a basketball court, for instance? Consider three of what might be called Coach DV's famous dictates, and think about their implications:

1. No lead is ever big enough,
2. Never celebrate early, and
3. Never *give* your opponents anything.

How do ideas like these get started? Where do they come from? How do they get such power, going from being mere notions to serious dictates that govern conduct and actions for decades after?

No Lead Is Ever Big Enough

Coach DV didn't learn this first grand dictate the hard way. In fact, he learned it in the most enjoyable way possible.

Very early in Coach DV's career, his team was playing against Beaver High School, in Pennsylvania. Beaver came out storming. They ran all over Coach DV's team. They came down the court, threw up a shot and—*Swish!*—it was good. Coach DV's team would go up the other end, take a good shot, but—*Thud!*—it missed. Over and over again, Beaver hit and DV's boys missed.

Coach DV called a timeout, followed by another and another. To no avail. Beaver could do no wrong. At the end of the first quarter, the score was something like 24-6, a drubbing unlike any Coach DV had ever experienced. The second quarter started out where the first had left off. Beaver, Beaver, Beaver. The score went to 34-8 when the Beaver coach decided to call off the dogs. He put his second team in, presumably to give them some playing time, to rest his stars, and very possibly to take it easy on a fellow coach. Why embarrass anyone, after all?

Why?

This game would give a special, career long meaning to the concept of embarrassment in basketball. Because once the Beaver starters were out of the game, you can probably guess what happened. Coach DV's team scored and Beaver missed, DV's team scored and Beaver missed. After four quick baskets, with the score at 34-16, the Beaver coach realized he needed "the dogs" back in there. By the time they got back in, it was 34-20, and suddenly the score didn't look so insurmountable.

Players whose shots began falling perfectly through the rim can't always continue such accuracy indefinitely. The Beaver shots started going awry. At the half, the score was a very surmountable 38-28. Coach DV's team went on to win by a comfortable margin.

After the game, Coach DV was almost apologetic to the Beaver coach. Somehow the game didn't seem quite right. His team had been overwhelmed until the opposing coach stopped the slaughter himself!

It was a mistake Coach DV would never make, not during his entire career. He would get accused of running up the score, of being unmerciful, of enjoying "rubbing it in," but he would never be guilty in forty years of allowing a beaten opponent to rise from the canvas and steal a win.

How could he sit there and keep applying a full court press with a huge margin on the scoreboard? The numbers 34-8 had much to do with it. They would linger in his brain for the rest of his career. In the end, his team won that Beaver game easily, all while clearing his bench and letting *his* reserves play!

Never Celebrate Early

This story would be better if Coach DV had once played on a team that lost a championship because of an early celebration. It is easy enough to imagine such a scenario: Team behind, seven seconds left, kid hits a seemingly winning basket, bench goes berserk with joy. Bench also spills out onto court, though time has not run out. Ref has no choice but to call a technical foul and the other team sinks two charity free throws—and wins title.

That *has* happened before, many times, in one form or another. In fact, football teams are supposed to get penalized fifteen yards anytime their celebrations spill out onto the field. Coach DV was particularly sensitive to that because he refereed high school football games for nearly twenty years. He refereed for (and had the respect of) coaches like Chuck Klausing, whose Braddock teams rolled up something like fifty consecutive victories, and Larry Bruno, DV's college roommate who coached and molded young Joe Namath into perhaps the best quarterback ever. Coach DV was a very conscientious official. Sideline celebrations set off warnings and made him itchy to grab and throw a red flag.

A rule is a rule, and as a referee, Coach DV called 'em as he saw 'em. Go on the field, you'll get a flag. It was that simple when Coach DV was a referee.

His football training, along with the periodic stories of technical fouls that turned jubilation into nightmares, set in stone Coach DV's attitude toward premature celebrations.

So, why would Coach DV seem to be yelling and screaming at his players—mad as hell—during a first quarter timeout after his team had just sprinted to a 10-0 lead? Because they ran off the court happy, "celebrating," as the fans went wild and cheered their excellent start.

Coach DV liked excellent starts. He always counseled his teams to "jump on 'em early." "Don't give 'em a chance to breathe," he would say. Don't let 'em get their confidence. By the time they get rid of their pre-game jitters, we want to be ahead by 15!"

Coach DV loved the 10-0 start, but his team better show a deadpan, all-business look on their way off the court. If he could have, Coach DV would have screamed at the whole crowd to shut the hell up. "We've only played three minutes of basketball! Now listen, dammit, listen!"

His team's attention had better be more earnest than ever,

because Coach DV would never be guilty of letting up or taking anything for granted. No way. What's 10 points? "Hell, teams catch up 10 points in the final minutes, and we still have a whole game to play."

Bet on Coach DV not to let anyone gloat over a small lead with 29 minutes left. If there was any time he was likely to grab a kid by the shirt or throw a kid off a team, it would be when he found himself going against the grain, the only one in the stadium who understood that leads are often temporary, that momentum shifts, that sports are fickle, and that the difference between victory and defeat is often an incredibly thin line.

There was no such thing as "savoring the moment" during a game.

Fans would look down at the bench and point and marvel and criticize. "Gawd, what's wrong with that madman? Look at how he's treating those kids. It's a wonder they are willing to play for him. My gawd, what do they have to do to satisfy him? You'd think by looking at him that his team was behind by 10, not ahead by 10."

They didn't realize how far off the mark they were.

If his team had suffered a 10-0 early drubbing, his demeanor might be entirely different, especially if nothing bad had happened other than the fact that his team's shots were not falling. (If the team were playing sloppily, however, *that* would be a different story!)

If the shots simply did not fall, he would calmly greet the dejected players coming back to the bench, nodding with his hands moving up and down at his chest, as if to say "Easy, easy, it's okay; it's no big thing. So they got a run; there's still a whole game to play. If you just go out there and play basketball, everything will be fine. These things happen sometimes. Don't worry about it, we can still kick their tails. We just have to go out there and play basketball."

His view was consistent. A ten point lead at the beginning of a game didn't necessarily mean anything at all. Sure, he worked hard to be on the high end of that score because, as he often urged, "Sometimes you can get a team early and they never recover." But his thinking didn't depart from the basic facts regardless of which team was ahead: leads are often temporary, momentum shifts, sports are fickle, and the difference between victory and defeat is often an incredibly thin line.

So you doggedly-yet-calmly go to work if you happen to find yourself behind, and you doggedly-yet-calmly go to work if you happen to find yourself ahead. When behind, a good coach will usually act very calm and reassuring to convey that panic is unnecessary. But when ahead, with excited rooters elated over a great spurt, a good coach usually has to battle the tide of jubilation to get the players to stay focused and to concentrate, so as not to lose the advantage they have gained.

It all makes perfect sense intellectually, but forty years of fans—particularly opponents' fans—thought Coach DV's antics warranted a place for him in an insane asylum instead of in the various sports halls of fame where his legacy now resides.

Never *Give* Your Opponents Anything

"This game is hard enough as it is," Coach DV often said. "Don't make it harder by giving anything away. You gotta make 'em work like hell for everything they get."

Probably the best example of this philosophy can be encapsulated through a brief halftime talk when my brother Dave was playing for Coach DV.

First of all, Coach DV was notorious for his halftime talks. This was his special time to go off, to really explode, for a couple of reasons:

1. All of the errors were fresh in his mind, and
2. He could still have an impact on the outcome of the game, if he was able to get his message across.

In other words, Coach DV was at his all-time best, his all-time angriest, his all-time "most colorful" during each halftime talk. Star players would come back years later and still be afraid to enter the locker room at halftime, even when Coach DV specifically invited them! Others would make it a point to listen outside the locker room door. In those locker rooms at halftime, Coach DV always defined and redefined the meaning of the word *intensity*. He was always—let me repeat—*always* enraged at halftime.

As a player, I sometimes felt able to let up a bit in the second quarter, having become distanced from his pre-game urgings. I knew that just ahead laid the halftime storm that would inevitably propel us to the top of our game at the start of the third quarter. It was almost like, "No use worrying what happens now; at halftime Coach DV will be so pissed and get us so revved up that we'll kick their asses in the third quarter." I'm not sure anyone thought in precisely those terms, but if it was possible at any time to let up, it would have been in anticipation of those incredibly motivating halftime harangues.

At the game in which my brother Dave was playing, Coach DV's team was facing a tough opponent which had been picked to be the main competition for the conference title. Coach DV's team had swept away most of the others in the race, so this was the grand showdown, the big game, supposedly one of those nip-and-tuckers that would go down to the wire and justify dozens of sports clichés. They could throw out the record books, give 500 percent, and know it would be a *war*. Only one thing went wrong.

Coach DV's team jumped all over its opponent and was strangling the spirit out of them by the time they caught their first breath. Ten-nothin', then twelve-nothin'. The first quarter ended and the other team still hadn't scored!

At halftime, as my brother and his teammates ran to the locker room, they carried an incredible 36-4 lead, and their opponents showed no signs (their coach included) of even wanting to return for the second half. It was a good old-fashioned ass-whipping of the first order; and it was one of those games when even a cautious, never-take-anything-for-granted coach like DV could see that the opponent had packed in their bags. They were conquered, and it was going to get worse and worse.

"What's he gonna yell about today?" one of my brother's friends asked, as they waited in the locker room for Coach DV to enter.

Coach had already counseled them at the quarter break and during three timeouts not to let up, and they had responded with nothing but a kind of bloodthirsty effort to pour it on. These guys wanted their points, didn't particularly like the other team, and had no mindset at all to let up one bit. Even Coach DV could sense that. It would be hollow and meaningless to rant and rave about letting up. This team was pouring it on.

So what would DV say? What could he possibly be angry about this time? His team had done *everything* he had asked of them. They had exceeded even his hopes, and he *knew* they couldn't wait to go out and do it again. So what could he say? Would this be the first halftime in his career, already twenty-five years along, that he would have to just praise his team and congratulate them and urge them to keep up the good work? His team had played the perfect game, and even Coach DV did not believe the other team could possibly mount a comeback. The only question really remaining in this game was how long Coach DV would stick to his concept that no lead is ever big enough.

"Today, finally, he ain't gonna be able to say nothin' to us." That was one player's prediction.

But Dave, Coach's son remained skeptical. "He's gotta find something. He *always* finds something."

Then Coach DV paced in—*stomped* in. As always, the room got totally quiet and still.

Coach DV opened with an afterthought: "Okay guys, it was a good half." Then he paused a moment, stirred up some rage, and blurted out, "But *gawt-darn-it!*"

He paced around some more, looking at the scorebook, holding up the scorebook, smacking the scorebook with the back of his hand and stoking his anger. And it was real anger, not manufactured. It was typical Coach DV, truly enraged at halftime, just like always.

Finally, after pacing and staring and smacking that book, his voice boomed from his stomach and twisted and shattered each player's hammer, anvil, and stirrup: *"Twenty-five years!"* he bellowed and paused, barely suppressing the anger so obviously welling up inside. *"Twenty-five years I've waited for a shutout!*—and you guys just *gave* them two baskets. That poor team *never* should have scored!"

He was serious.

19.
ETIQUETTE AND EVERY-TIME REINFORCEMENT

Congratulations on a tremendous year . . . You continue to inspire young men to do their best . . . I hope that in my seventeen years of coaching I inspired one young man as much as you have inspired a multitude of young men . . . I wish there was some way it could be arranged that you would one day coach my three sons.

— Coach John Hince
Former Coach DV player

IT'S TERRIBLE TO HAVE A MAN LIKE THAT WORKING WITH YOUNG KIDS. NO WONDER THERE'S PROBLEMS IN THE SCHOOLS.

Etiquette and Every-Time Reinforcement

Most coaches get criticized—and fired—for losing too much. Most of Coach DV's problems and the criticism directed at him down through the years resulted from winning too much. Or rather, from winning too big. From winning by margins considered by some to be unrespectable.

Imagine it. Coach DV's team is ahead by 40 points. It's the third quarter. All of his starters are in the game playing a killer full-court press, swarming over their hapless foes. Three, four, five straight times the other team fails to even cross mid court before Coach DV's team steals the ball and lays it in for easy baskets. The score mounts. The pressure defense is unrelenting. Suddenly, the other team throws a long pass. DV's defender down the court is slow reacting, and instead of intercepting the pass, he runs into the receiver.

Tweet!

The defender is whistled for a foul, and Coach DV is livid. He leaps from the bench and calls a timeout. Before his players can even get to the bench, he is already chewing them out, particularly the kid who just allowed a fifty-foot pass to be caught.

"You clumsy oaf," Coach DV says, so loudly that most of the crowd hears him. "You can't stand back there like a dumb gazook. What if we were playing a *real* team?"

Coach DV didn't intend that to be an insult to the other team or to their fans. He was totally serious. This wasn't a "real" team. They didn't have players who worked hard all summer to improve their skills. They didn't have kids who made 500 shots a day or went to camps or played together each summer evening. They were "nice boys who were participating in a school activity."

Nevertheless, the point was, regardless of the conditions or the opponent, a basketball player should *never* allow a fifty-foot pass to be caught. As Coach DV said, "If you were just *half* awake, you had time to get over there to catch *that*. They threw that ball right to you, but you didn't want it."

Some fans didn't see it that way, and administrators didn't necessarily see it that way either. Those people were more likely to be focused on entirely different issues.

"What's wrong with that maniac? They have a 40 point lead and he's chewing out those kids and calling them names."

"Why is he keeping up a full-court press? He just wants to rub it in."

"All he cares about is publicity. He thinks if his team rolls up big scores, people will think he's a good coach."

"He always tries to embarrass the other team. I'm not staying for this. This is the poorest example of sportsmanship I have ever witnessed. The principal of that school is going to hear about this. It's terrible to have a man like that working with young kids. No wonder there's problems in the schools with people like that teaching our kids."

"What goes around comes around. Wait till we have a better team; see how *he* likes it."

Yes, *see* how he *would* like it!

Not very many coaches or teams ever managed to run up a score on Coach DV. They were happy if they were able to win at all. No coach who opposed him more than twice had a winning record against Coach DV, and very few coaches ever had the luxury of deciding whether or not to put reserves in.

Coach DV never expected or wanted mercy. He didn't think that was what the game was all about. The game was about doing the best you could. You would expect the opponents to do the best they could. Both teams try to do as well as they can. That means both teams try to score as many points as they can.

Coach DV never quite understood all the fuss about "sports etiquette." In fact, he really didn't know what it was.

Consider the kinds of questions Coach DV *did* think about:

What is a respectable margin of victory? Why would any coaches want to lose by just 20 if they were actually 60 points worse than the other team? What joy or satisfaction would they get from that "respectable" score if it had come as a gift, instead of earned? How would you even know if you had improved, assuming there was a rematch later in the season, if the superior team just chose to win by 20 both times? Wouldn't *that* be more humiliating to a weak team than giving them the opportunity to be proud of getting each point? Wouldn't they feel more respect and pride in themselves by working hard and losing the second time by only 40, instead of just getting those two losses by 20, never knowing what points they were earning and what points were gifts?

Furthermore, what exactly is point-shaving? If a coach or player knowingly controls the margin of victory (to benefit from gambling), this is considered a scandalous crime which destroys the whole meaning and purpose of sports. But how much different is it, when a coach or team controls the margin of victory because of someone's skewed notion of respectability?

Is it even *fair* to beat a team by 20 if you are really 40 points better? (This question has broad implications.) Why should a group of kids who practice all summer and commit themselves to basketball and make personal sacrifices, average just a few more points per game than others who don't practice in the off-season and don't make sacrifices?

If you beat a team only 60-40, your five guys will average 12 points for the game, while the other team's players will average 8. Not much of a difference, especially once other games are added in. If you beat a team 100-40, the difference is more compelling. You have five guys averaging 20 points; they have five guys averaging 8. *That* is a difference that reflects realistically the two teams' very different commitments to basketball.

When it comes time to get awards and to choose all-conference or regional all-star teams, those differences matter. If there isn't a clear difference in performance statistics, selection committees and newspaper reporters are going to spread the awards and choose the best player on that 40-point team over two or three players who are clearly better on that 60-point team. What's fair about *that*? Face it, they are much less likely to make those kinds of decisions to the detriment of the players on a team that has demonstrated overwhelming superiority.

The fairness issue doesn't end there either. Coach DV had a strong sense of the fact that a committed kid spends, in the off-season, about an hour for every minute of game time that exists during a season. If this kid gets taken out of a game and plays only half the time, that means he's getting only a half minute in return for his hour of effort.

Is it fair to penalize a kid who has worked hard, and to reduce his playing time and his point production, just because some other kids haven't made the same commitment? Coach DV didn't think so. He wanted his players to be able to build up their scoring averages in the easy games so they would not be tempted to be selfish and to worry about things like that in the tougher games.

Unselfishness and good team play are essential to winning basketball. One way to help foster that is to keep everyone's statistics up, particularly way above others who are not very good players.

Coach DV would say often, "It's nice for your grandparents to read about you in the papers. They won't know you were playing the Little Sisters of the Poor!"

He and his players enjoyed the humor but recognized the truth in it, too. Basketball players like seeing their names in the papers, and they like piling up statistics. Coach DV wanted to reward the players who had worked hard and who had reached a level where they deserved acclaim for their skills.

As far as Coach DV was concerned, it was up to the *other* coach and to the *other* team to keep the score respectable; it was not up to him and his team. He wanted his players to score as many points as their skills enabled them to score. That seemed appropriate. It seemed right. It seemed like *real* sportsmanship. The score should reflect the *actual* difference in the skills of the two teams.

As for "that maniac" yelling at his team when 40 points ahead and continuing to apply an aggressive full court press . . .

People who are not winners by nature don't readily comprehend the concept of "every time reinforcement." Every time reinforcement is a hallmark of those few people who truly understand what it takes to be successful in highly competitive environments.

If there was one prime quality which set Coach DV in a very select group, above literally millions of other coaches throughout the world and throughout history, it would have to be his ability—call it incredible energy and commitment—to correct every error he ever saw for forty years. Ahead by 40, behind by 40, in games, in practice, with a headache, with a sore throat . . . the environment was simply *not* a factor. In the face of an error, the score at the time was absolutely irrelevant to him. An error must be corrected to prevent its recurrence. Fail to correct an error and you will see it again—and be responsible for it!

Great coaches see all events as though they are playing against champions or about to play champions. That is the *only* way to coach a team to prepare its players to be champions. This may make it clearer why a coach like DV would have so much trouble accepting a suggestion from a fan. The fan that could wonder about yelling at a kid whose team enjoyed a 40-point lead simply had no concept of what championship coaching is all about. To have to consider the score and other outside factors before correcting an error would be nearly impossible.

If you asked Coach DV how he mustered the energy to correct all those errors all the time, he would answer modestly and sincerely, "I wouldn't be smart enough to figure out all those gray areas: when to correct, when not to correct. I'm not that intelligent. It's easier for me if I just correct them all. Then I don't have to worry about the score or who has a headache or problems at home."

So why keep applying a full-court press? Couldn't he have his team just drop back into a zone?

He *could*. But why would he? His teams pressed as a standard. If they were playing a game, it wouldn't make sense to switch to a defense that they didn't often use. The idea is to maximize every minute. There are many things a coach would like to tell a team and have them work on, but there just isn't time. So, drop back in a defense they didn't need practice on? The idea is wasteful. It flies in the face of everything else they did everyday in practice. Maximize time. Strive to improve. Use every second and every circumstance to get a little bit better.

If you were talking about one of Coach DV's teams that played zone or played his matchup defense, then of course they could drop back and work on that. But how could he ask one of his pressing teams to drop back? That thought would not have come to his mind.

The thought that *would* occur to him was: "Okay boys, this team is lousy. They should *never* get the ball over mid court on you. Go out there and don't let them complete a pass!"

Time well spent? You betcha! Instead of a wasted game—a laugher against a team that doesn't belong in the same gym with you—suddenly he has created a fierce competition that can indeed help you get better. When your goal is not to allow a completed pass, or at least not to allow the ball to cross mid court, each player must be on his toes the whole time, nervous, worried, strung tight, determined.

When you are trying to shut a team out, play does not get sloppy and nothing seems easy. The time is maximized, as it has to be, if you are hoping to win championships.

But wait a minute, you might say. Don't the reserves want to play, too? Don't they want to score, too? Don't their grandmothers want to read about *them* in the papers, too?

Of course. But Coach DV didn't believe that players should get undeserved credit on the coattails of others. The real value of credit, publicity, and recognition is felt only if it is deserved.

So, put in the reserves? Give them a chance to play?

Occasionally, maybe. But not as a top priority. If they wanted recognition from basketball, they could get it. But they should want *real* recognition, Coach DV thought, the kind that comes from practicing and being among those truly responsible for the team's success. The reserves, therefore, should be young players whose time was in the future.

The people who should get the playing time now where those who worked and earned the right to play.

Sure, it would be nice to put the whole school in the game, Coach DV thought. But a basketball game isn't long enough for a whole school to get to play. It isn't even long enough for fifteen kids to get enjoyment from playing.

Coach DV believed that a basketball team should have seven or eight players on it, and those seven or eight would play all the time. He would substitute often and impulsively; there wouldn't be many games when only the first five started and played the whole time. If he had confidence in two or three players on the bench, they might play even more than the starters. But he never wanted to have to try to satisfy fifteen players. It was just too many. Instead, his teams always practiced alongside the junior varsity team. That way, his varsity team had people to practice against. Plus, Coach DV could personally guide the development of the young players on their way up to his team.

On his teams, there wasn't usually the need to give playing time to kids who practiced but didn't get to play. His reserves had already played in the junior varsity game earlier in the evening. He chose two or three of them to dress out in case they were needed because of injuries or foul trouble. Sometimes he would use them in the varsity game, either out of anger or curiosity, but not because he had to in order to keep them happy. He didn't want the burden of having to keep too many kids happy. Trying to keep fifteen basketball players happy on one team was like trying to give seven birthday presents to fifteen people. Cut all those gifts in half and no one would have anything but a broken toy. Better to give seven a nice gift. He'd rather do that and take his chances on later injuries, foul trouble, flunk outs, and other eligibility problems. He would rather worry about those possibilities than start a season knowing he couldn't please all the players on the team.

20.
WASTED TIMEOUTS, GRABBY-GRABBY, AND YOU CAN BEAT ANYBODY

Just a note of congratulatory remarks about your great team and also your approach to the wonderful game of basketball. It surely was a revelation to watch a group of boys perform with such wonderful poise and self-assurance throughout the tournament. I thought your passing was superb, which I believe was the key point of your philosophy to the game. I was especially pleased that we do have those in the game that teach maneuverability, great defense, and tremendous strategy.

— Paul Birch Duquesne
All-American and pro star

What the hell are you guys doing? You lined up like a bunch of fracking orphans waiting in a breadline. You weren't ready to get that ball.

Wasted Timeouts, Grabby-Grabby, and You Can Beat Anybody

Hall of Fame coach Dean Smith, who won twenty games per season for twenty-five consecutive years at the University of North Carolina, has had widespread impact with his innovations and success. For example, he taught coaches all over the world to save their timeouts until the end of games so they could be used to stop the clock and mount a late comeback.

Coach DV and Dean Smith were personal friends for more than twenty-five years. Coach DV admired Coach Smith and was very aware of his philosophies, his innovations, and his successes. Coach DV respected everything Coach Smith did and would never argue that his own methods were as thought-out or as statistically sound as Coach Smith's. Nevertheless, those same sound ideas wouldn't influence Coach DV when his instincts told him to do something different.

For example, it was not unusual for Coach DV to spend one of his precious timeouts only two seconds after tip-off. The jump ball would start the game, and the tap might go out of bounds. It might not be clear who would get possession, or perhaps there would have to be a re-jump. Coach DV would erupt off the bench, angry as hell, and in that insuppressible growl coming deep from his gut he would demand a timeout.

That would get the fans buzzing all over an arena. What had happened? What had they missed? Was there a fight or an elbow thrown? What could possibly have happened in two seconds to enrage that coach and get him to use a timeout?

In familiar fashion, Coach DV would growl and bark before his team ever reached the bench. He did not stand to the side calmly and consult with his assistants first, as is the habit of most successful coaches like Dean Smith. Not on your life. Coach DV was emoting. There was no time for consultation.

"What the hell are you guys doing?" he would say. "You lined up like a bunch of fracking orphans waiting in a breadline. You weren't ready to get that ball." He would look alternately at one player after another. "*You* weren't ready to get the ball! You were standing back on your heels! You weren't on your toes!

"And you, you were ready, Joe. But you didn't help these poor simps. You can't just be ready yourself. We went out there to just *give* them a lay-up. We're just fortunate they didn't want to take it because we were handing it to them. You can't play basketball like that. You gotta play. Gawt-darn-it, are you gonna play?"

It was one of those questions that demanded an answer because players knew he was very willing to replace them all with the reserves—or maybe with the jayvees—in order to make his point. But he would generally get some nods and some *Yes, Coach*es, so he wouldn't take out the whole starting team. He was sure as hell willing to do that, since he had done it before many times.

"Well, *play* then!" he would say.

If anyone, like an assistant, had been consulted or had offered that it might not be a wise decision to use up a timeout with only two seconds gone and the score 0-0, Coach DV would have barked out in disgust: "Bull shit! I'm not going to sit here and watch that crap. If we come to play like that, we won't need any gawt-darn timeouts at the end. We'll be so gawt-darn far behind it won't matter."

"But Coach, don't you want to save your timeouts like Dean Smith does?"

"He can do that. He coaches college players. I don't have that luxury. I got a bunch of gawt-darn gazooks standing there like fairies wanting to *give* the game away. I can't afford to do that crap. I'd like to. Hell yeah, I'd like to coach like Dean Smith. I just can't afford it. *He* doesn't have to coach a bunch of *gawt-darn* fairies."

If you or if a reporter asked him, after the heat of the action and in the calm of a victorious locker room, his answer would be a bit different, but not much.

"I know you're supposed to save timeouts. Coach Smith wouldn't use one at the beginning like that. But I'm not Coach Smith. I don't teach as well. I have to do things my way. I just have to get the guys ready to play. If I think they aren't ready, then I have to do something. I'd like to be able to save timeouts like Coach Smith does, but I just can't. Not when I see our guys standing out there like a bunch of fairies. *Ohhhh!* That gets ya!"

There is more to it than that, however. If the opposing coach happened to look over, or a young assistant or an opposing fan, or if Coach DV overheard someone claim they had gotten some sort of early advantage by forcing him to use one of his timeouts (the kind of thing that TV commentators are fond of pointing out) Coach DV would display a totally different way of thinking.

"Frack that horseshit. We don't need any gawt-darn timeouts. They can have ours. I'm just doing this to raise hell. Advantage for them? Shit! You don't get any points for timeouts. That's just to make you think you're doing something or to make the administrators think you're earning your pay. You don't need timeouts, you need to play basketball. That's all. You just gotta play ball. You just gotta cut out all the crap and play ball!"

The attitude Coach DV always conveyed to his players was, "Hell yes, I'm willing to use a timeout with two seconds gone. I'm under no illusions. It doesn't matter what the hell I say over here. Sure, I can scream and holler. But the game is won out there. *You guys just have to play ball.*"

The explanation could go on. In that quick-trigger anger, there was a consistent, winning attitude that wasn't always obvious to fans but which was very compelling in action.

Incredibly, not once in Coach DV's career was he or anyone else ever able to point out a time when, had he saved one more timeout, the game could have been turned around. Maybe one could have, of course, but there are no glaring examples. It goes back to instinct. In the tough games, the really big games, players are likely to catch the fire of the moment; the chances of them lining up for the jump ball "like a bunch of fairies" are slim. In reality, Coach DV may never have called one of his two-second timeouts against a team where every tiny advantage would end up mattering.

His use of timeouts frequently contradicted conventional wisdom, but he called every one of them with a definite purpose in mind and a clear view of what had to be done. Though always amiable prior to tip-off and generally friendly after a game, Coach DV was immersed emotionally in every play of the competition.

In retrospect, his "wasted" timeouts were actually astute psychological ploys, though Coach DV would never have claimed that. He was just pissed! When you really examined them, these timeouts always seemed to happen at the beginning of games when circumstances and Coach DV's players were ripe for an upset. They came almost always against so-called "easy" teams when Coach DV sensed that things had to be stirred up. *No one* could do it better. Every coach and good fan realizes that weak teams should never be taken lightly because every year so-called good teams lose games to inferior teams. But players can't get "up" for every game, so how does a good coach prevent letdowns and upsets?

Coach DV was the master at avoiding upsets. If he didn't teach or prepare or scout or use timeouts as well as Dean Smith, he probably went one better than Smith in this category. Upsets hardly *ever* happened to Coach DV. He despised the idea of being upset by an inferior team. He took no one lightly, although you would never pick that up from his instructions to his players during a halftime.

"You can't let this group of little kids beat you. They are probably nice boys, but they aren't *bas*ketball players . . . If you lose to this bunch of farmers you should be ashamed to show your face in school tomorrow . . . These little kids couldn't beat my grandmother . . . These jumbrones, they are just a bunch of wild men who have no idea how to play this game . . . They aren't worth a crap; they don't have one guy who could play on *our* team but they're beating your tails . . . These are thin, scrawny kids from Hampton; you can't lose to thin, scrawny kids from Hampton . . . This team couldn't beat a bunch of old ladies . . . They don't play basketball, they just throw the ball at the basket

. . . They couldn't punch their way out of a paper bag . . ."

Before or after a game, talking to the opposing coach or to the players on the opposing team, Coach DV was always highly complimentary. He would point out specific, good things that the players or the coach had done, and his admiration for those things was very sincere and always appreciated by whomever he was addressing. But in his own locker room, without changing his tune, the spin on the story would be quite different.

What was expressed to an opposing player as "You did a nice job, son; that's a good shot you have," to his own team was changed to "You can't let that little kid score! He can do *one* thing. His parents paved his driveway and put up a basket and he stands out there and shoots, and he can shoot. So you guys *let* him stand there and shoot. We're so gawt-darn dumb. If you make him do anything else, he'll fall all over the place. He's no *bas*ketball player, but he sure as hell isn't gonna know that if you let him just stand there doing the only thing he *can* do!"

Coach DV could spot weaknesses from miles away, and he spotted them in almost everyone. There were very few real *bas*ketball players, and when he saw one, he truly did admire that kid. A *bas*ketball player was a kid who didn't crap around, who ran fast, stayed constantly on the move, and made everything look easy because he didn't try to do difficult things. He just did everything right, always a couple of steps ahead of everyone else.

The other 99.9 percent of the players, the non-basketball players, got no respect from Coach DV when he was disgusted with his team at halftime. "That thin little kid . . . that clumsy oaf . . . that fat tub . . . that poor simp . . . that nice boy . . . that fine young lad . . . that bunch of orphans . . . those wild men from Borneo . . . that bunch of screaming ninnies . . . those dumb gazooks—*they don't know how to play basketball!*"

In case any of his players felt any sense of intimidation after reading about some star on the other team, Coach DV would quickly dispel that feeling. "Star? That's no star. That's what they write in the paper. That kid can't play basketball—unless you *let* him."

One of Coach DV's greatest gifts as a coach was his ability to convey to his players, *"You can beat anyone."*

It was never a rah-rah, "you can do it, you can do it" kind of urging. He *never* counseled his players to have confidence. He never told them that they had to believe in themselves. The issue *never* even came up.

The only issue that mattered was playing basketball. If you go out there and just play basketball, you can beat anyone. The explanation, coupled with Coach DV's special brand of disgust as he imparted his ideas, was compelling. It left no player with any doubt.

"Hell yeah, they're good," he'd say. "But not if you play basketball. High school kids *love to make mistakes*, and they will make plenty if *you* play basketball and give them the opportunity. But you have to give them the opportunity. You can't just stand around. If you stand around, sure they're good. Everyone's an All-American when you stand around and crap around. But you can't let 'em be All-Americans; you gotta play basketball."

He had other thoughts about so-called unbeatable teams and reported superstars.

"Horseshit. At the end of the game, their coach will be happy if they shoot 55 percent and so will their superstar. They will be *happy with 55 percent!*

"Do you know what that means, boys? Do you understand? It means, if you don't crap around, all we have to do is play basketball and shoot 60 percent, and we'll win. As long as you don't *give* them baskets and throw the ball away, we can beat them even though they are *happy* with their performance. If we play basketball and make them work, make them earn everything and don't just give them baskets, we'll be okay."

"We'll be okay," he would say, but he meant, "We can beat their ass and give them the surprise of their lives—if we will just play basketball."

Players knew what playing basketball meant. It meant simply following those four basic rules: move, pass to each other, don't shoot until you get an easy one, and make them work like hell for everything they get. It was very simple. It was also extremely effective psychologically.

As a player, you never had to worry—and you never did worry—about how good *they* were. Your only worry was whether or not you would do what you were supposed to do. Execute. Run. Play smart. Play hard. Be alert. That's all Coach DV ever wanted. If you gave it, if you satisfied him, you could beat anyone.

"Oh sure, he's 6'10". He'll score some points," he would say. "But we don't need to hold him scoreless to win. We just have to make sure we don't give him any."

Coach DV was always aware that even great players have bad games. He himself was a great player, and he had vivid recollections of a couple of passes he threw away in a big game at Geneva College back in the Forties. He also remembered well a heralded scoring duel between him and a player from a rival school. Coach DV won 4-3!

Great players don't always play great. "Sure he's great, but that's no reason he has to play great against us. Let's make this one of his *off* nights. Let's make him work like hell for everything he gets. Let's *help* him have an off night!"

"*Help* stars have off nights . . . *Give* teams the opportunity to make mistakes . . . *Give* the "buzhokes" some rope and let them hang themselves . . . Let wild men shoot." All of those things were just common sense to Coach DV. They were part of playing basketball the way the game is supposed to be played. You don't bow down to a star; you make him prove he's a star every second of every play. You don't hope the other team makes mistakes; you pressure them and hound them and bother them and get in their way and prevent them from doing all of the things they are comfortable doing; and you provide them opportunities to play worse than usual.

"We don't mind them leaving here thinking they could have beaten us if only they had not had a bad day. You see, boys, people don't understand; they love to make excuses. If we make it easy for them to make mistakes, they will usually make mistakes, and they will think they did it on their own. That's fine. It's okay if they think that. They don't need to know we had anything to do with it. All we care about is beating them."

You can beat anybody. The message came through loud and clear. So clear, Coach DV rarely spent time on scouting his opponents. Just about everything he needed to know he could get from a newspaper, from almost any fan, and from watching them warm up for a few minutes.

Which of their players are good outside shooters? Which of their players do most of their scoring? Are any of them left-handed? That's about all Coach DV wanted to know.

Once, late in his career, Coach DV decided that perhaps he should scout an upcoming opponent. He watched only half their game before departing. When he got home, he realized he had left his notes somewhere at the gym. It probably didn't matter; in all likelihood he had written little down.

While other great coaches watched film after film and perhaps scouted their opponents several times, Coach DV ignored that kind of stuff. "I'm not worried about them. I'm worried about us. If we play basketball, we'll be fine regardless of what they have. And if we don't . . ." Nothing more needed to be said.

Coach DV wasn't even particularly concerned about knowing what defense they played. If they played zone, he would use his zone attack: move the ball, get easy shots. If they played man to-man, he would use his man offense: move fast, make easy passes, get easy shots. If they pressed, take it up court, don't crap around.

If you "play basketball" there is only really one defense. There are no zones, no mans, no presses. Just a scramble to try to prevent an easy basket.

When one man beats another man, someone has to pick him up. Then, it's 5-on-4 for the offense. While the man picking up has to move quickly and make it tough for the player with the ball, the man beaten has to recover or immediately find a loose player so that the 5-on-4 reverts to 5-on-5.

It was the same for both teams. Many coaches can talk about intricate players and X's and O's all night. Coach DV hated talking about X's and O's with coaches; he thought it all boiled down to the player with the ball, how he reacts, and how the rest of the players play out the 5-on-4 that happens over and over again in ever-changing ways.

What's all the fuss over whether a team begins in a 1-3-1 or a 2-3 or a pressure man or a sagging zone? It's all going to boil down to the idea of gaining an advantage and then scoring on that 5-on-4, which is, again, nothing but *playing basketball.*

If you don't crap around, if you are alert, if you anticipate what is going to happen, if you come to meet the ball, if you are decisive, if you can throw and catch, if you can see the open man . . . these were the ingredients of basketball that mattered to Coach DV. It didn't matter how many plays some team had or how many books were written about the game. This was Coach DV's clear, simple understanding of roundball.

He didn't try to teach the game piece by piece. As he was always quick to say he "didn't know how." What he did was impart a sense of the game, a compelling attitude, toughness, and alertness.

It didn't bother him in the least that every team he ever played knew exactly what he was going to do. They knew his team's simple offensive continuity; they knew what defense he would play. It didn't matter. Coach DV wasn't into surprises. He never tried to surprise anyone, and he never felt his team could be surprised.

"Hell, what's a surprise? If they play without the lights on or if they sneak in two extra players or if they have trampolines on the court, *those* would be surprises. But if they just bring five guys, there's not all that much anyone can do. If they try to double-team, you just have to hit the open man. If they don't, then you have to beat them one to one, and if they pick up well, you have to hit the open man. There aren't many secrets to this game. You just have to play basketball."

A young coach trying to imitate Coach DV's style would have difficulty. He would miss all sorts of elements of "playing basketball" that Coach DV knew and reinforced intuitively. For example, although he said "all you have to do is hit the open man," that man has to be in just the right position to be ready to catch the pass so a defender cannot intercept it. If the four players without the ball aren't spaced well, three defenders can guard all four. As a result, good coaches will typically talk about spacing. I don't think Coach DV ever did. His teaching of spacing came in other forms.

"Son, what the hell are you doing way over there? Don't you see the ball here? Doesn't it occur to you that this man might go in here?" At times like this, his voice was likely to be sarcastic and ominously calm. "Isn't it likely that someone might pick up this young lad? Well, if those two very likely things happen, then this poor lad is going to need someone to pass to. Is there any reason that person couldn't be *you*? Well then get there, young boy, nice boy, nice young lad." The normal tone of disgust would usually follow. "You have so much to learn about this game. You can't stand in Timbuktu when one of your teammates starts driving to the basket. Oh my, oh my, oh my. *Get over there!*"

The kid may not have learned a clear sense of spacing, but you can be sure that the next time the ball went driving in from that other side, the kid would be getting his body closer to the play, ready to receive a pass!

In the same way, when Coach DV would see two of his players standing close together, he would stop everything, and—maybe, if the other players were lucky—he would even make everyone laugh. In seeming seriousness, after he had made everyone stop, he would walk quickly to that place where the two players were standing. Sometimes he would sniff the air like a bloodhound.

"Does he have something in his pocket?" Coach DV might ask. The players would have no idea what he was talking about or getting at. "You weren't playing with his thing, were you?"

What? they would wonder.

"Do you like the way he smells?"

The players were confused, except maybe for a senior or two who had seen this act once before.

"Well, if you're not sniffing him or playing with his thing, *what the hell are you doing standing beside him?* There sure as hell isn't any *basketball* reason for standing beside him. Of course, I had to assume you were playing grabby-grabby with each other!"

He might turn his attention to the better of the two players, the one who had actually been in good position except for the fact that the other player had come close. "You're not a little different, are you?" Coach would say, in a very calm, even voice (inquiring about the kid's sexual preference, you might say).

"No, Coach."

"Then tell him next time to get the hell outta there, or you get the hell outta there. You can't stand there together like you're playing grabby-grabby. This is a *bas*ketball team. If two of you stand together, one of their guys can guard both of you. Can't you see that?"

"Yes, Coach."

"Well then, do it. I don't like hollering at you or making fun of you, boys, but you gotta play this game. I don't ask you to learn a bunch of trick plays. We don't have anything complicated. I don't know anything complicated. I can't teach anything complicated. And I don't like anything complicated. I don't *want* anything complicated. All I'm asking you to do is play like human beings. You don't *ever* stand together like that in a basketball game. Do you understand?"

Usually, they understood. It's called spacing, and I suspect that Coach DV got his point across better than most coaches. That is, he got his players to execute better than most coaches, though his methods or explanations would hardly be approved by the World Coaches Federation.

21.
PURITY:
CORRECTING THE OTHER TEAM AND WAR ON THE BEACHES

DV ran us until my legs were fifty pounds heavier. Then he kept running us *some more . . . When the game arrived, we forgot about our gripes; we knew we were a prepared team. We were conditioned to play to the best of our ability.*

— Ken Rankin
Former Coach DV player

BE SURE OF THIS. THAT VOICE, THAT ANGER, EVERYTHING ABOUT THAT INTENSE, COMPETITIVE DEMEANOR LEFT ZERO SPACE FOR SMIRKS AND FOR QUESTIONS LIKE "WHO THE HELL DO YOU THINK YOU ARE?"

Purity: Correcting the Other Team and War on the Beaches

"Son, cut out that dribbling and pass the ball!" Coach DV blurted out, startling the player with the ball, confusing him, getting his parents very irritated, and even causing some administrators to become involved.

Why such a fuss about a simple command like that?

Well, for starters, you have to realize that Coach DV's commands weren't like any others. His voice was gruffer and harsher than nearly anyone else's. It reached out and grabbed you, unlike others. It was more intense, more emotion-packed. When Coach DV yelled at someone, there was real power—a kind of awesome force behind it that was truly scary, particularly for people who weren't used to it. A kid being reprimanded by someone like Coach DV just couldn't ignore it and pretend it never happened. Coach DV's rage, aimed at you, would grab you by the collar bone, jerk you to attention, and shake you, slap you, pulverize you.

Maybe that is overstating it. But it is difficult to explain in words on a page the impact that a forceful person with a booming voice and a taut intensity can have when he is angry and blurts out his irritation.

Still, why all the fuss about Coach DV yelling at a kid to cut out that dribbling and pass the ball?

The kid was on the other team!

This incident, which happened more than once, brings to mind another. The president of the Little League Baseball Association in our town once walked from the bleachers to the edge of the field at a crucial time in a game and said, in an authoritative adult voice, "Son, let me see that ball!"

The pitcher, responding to authority as 12-year-olds in small towns are taught to do, tossed the ball to the president. But the president, whose son played on the team at bat, moved out of the way and the ball rolled into the bleachers, permitting two runs to score!

Can you believe it? The president claimed that he was wearing no official badge or uniform, that he had acted as a mere fan, drawing the pitcher into a stupid error. According to him, it was the coach's fault that he hadn't taught his players to ignore outside distractions.

The young umpire was inclined to send the runners back to their bases and disallow the runs, but the president had hired the umpire! He claimed it would be breaking a rule. "A rule is a rule," he said. "What would this league come to without a commitment to obey the rules?"

So the two runs stood. A meeting was called. The league nearly broke up. Parents were irate. It just wasn't right for an adult, particularly the president of the League, to bamboozle a youngster as he did. Kids in small towns were taught to respect authority. What kind of values could they expect these kids to develop if the adults couldn't be trusted?

They had a point, of course. The action of that president was ridiculous. Had *my* team been up to bat when that happened, Coach DV would have had that president's head! There's no way those runs would have scored had Coach DV been in the crowd that day. In fact, there's no way those two runs would have scored regardless of which team Coach DV was pulling for.

That is what clearly separated Coach DV's actions from those of adults trying to look for angles and inject themselves into kids' games.

Parents and administrators charged that Coach DV had yelled at that kid dribbling the ball in order to confuse and distract him in the way that the Little League president had done.

But they couldn't have been further from the truth. There was only one thing that motivated Coach DV to yell at a kid with a basketball in his hands: true love for the game of basketball and the spontaneous feeling that the kid was "fracking up the game" and hurting himself in the process. Basketball, according to Coach DV, was such a great game with so many possibilities (for growth, for enjoyment, for friendship, for manhood) that he simply couldn't tolerate seeing a kid miss all that.

"You don't play basketball like that, son. If your coach isn't going to do it, someone has to teach you how to play this game!"

Coach DV loved sports and competition, and he truly appreciated and admired good athletes and outstanding athletic performances.

If a kid, playing against his team, made an outstanding play, it wasn't at all abnormal for Coach DV to compliment him. This was not done to gain some sort of advantage or to soften the kid up. It was heart-felt, emotion-filled, sincere appreciation.

In fact, more often than actually complimenting the opponent directly, Coach DV would compliment the opponent to his own team. "You see, boys? *That's* how you play basketball!" Admittedly, the tone didn't always remain admiring in these situations. Usually it would become, "How come *he* knows how to play like that and *we* don't? Why can't you guys play like that? Is that so hard? Watch him, boys. Someone taught that kid how to play the game."

When Coach DV yelled at the kid to pass the ball instead of dribbling, he had just one thought in his mind: that kid dribbled too much and needed to pass the ball!

When accused by a parent of trying to use psychology on the kid, Coach DV blew up all over. "That's ridiculous. First of all, I'm not smart enough to use psychology. And second, ma'am, with all due respect, we didn't need psychology to beat your poor team. Your team has a lot of nice boys on it, but they aren't *bas*ketball players. And your coach is a nice young guy and he seems to mean well. He's trying, but he's not too experienced. I was just trying to help, ma'am."

People couldn't believe it. No doubt they were aware of Coach DV's reputation and the respect other coaches had for him. Rival coaches might claim Coach DV knew every trick in the book because that was their way of seeing it, but actually they misunderstood. In truth, Coach DV wasn't interested in tricks. He had one interest: good basketball played hard, played intensely, played to win. Period. His mind didn't work at all like the president of that Little League association.

When his principal called him in to discuss the basketball incident, Coach DV again became irate. How could the principal be so gawt-darn dumb, too? He knew Coach DV. He watched him at every game. Surely he could *see* that Coach DV had never shown the slightest inclination to confuse opposing players with psychology. Coach DV could tolerate the parents of some other team not understanding him or his intentions, but his own principal? It didn't give him much respect for administrators.

The principal, eager to please everyone and smooth over the situation, said he wasn't accusing Coach DV of anything. He just wanted to discuss the matter.

"Gawt-darn-it, John, what the hell is there to discuss?" Coach DV would say. "Tell them what the hell really happened and don't bother me with this—and don't bother yourself with it either. We all have more important things to worry about than some grandmother who thinks her grandson was psyched out by another team's coach. If you think I did that, just fire me, John. I don't have time for this horseshit."

The principal would necessarily tread lightly. He wasn't very used to tough, high-intensity people himself. He was more inclined, like the parent whom Coach called a grandmother, to wonder what Coach DV had meant by his comments.

"I meant what the hell I said, John, the way I always do. Now what the hell do *you* mean?"

The principal would shuffle off trying to explain that he had just wanted to resolve the matter, but Coach DV wouldn't give him any satisfaction. There was nothing to resolve. This was total horseshit, that's all, and he didn't have time for it. Didn't the principal notice that every day after school, lines of students waited outside Coach DV's classroom door for their turn to talk with him? Coach DV cared as intensely about people as he cared about good basketball. High school kids caught on to that and gravitated to him.

Coach DV served as an unofficial guidance counselor. He

spent many, many hours after school and during free periods and study halls talking to kids about their problems, their home lives, their parents, their boyfriends. He listened and cared and tried to help with the same intensity that he coached basketball.

How in the hell could the principal not know that Coach DV would be the last one in the world to try to psych out a kid on a basketball court? There was just no way he would do that.

Generally, players on opposing teams, particularly the good players, loved Coach DV. They warmed to his sincere compliments and his insight. His compliments reached people because they hit the mark and were accompanied by real appreciation and admiration that a person could feel. Coach DV didn't issue compliments perfunctorily, as courtesies. But he would go out of his way to express his appreciation whenever an athlete, coach, or any other person had done something to evoke his admiration.

Why correct a player on another team?

He really did care about people and about the game. He hated to see young kids expending their efforts without guidance or purpose. He had a strong sense of what sports done right could be and how dismal, irritating, and unfulfilling sports could be when done wrong.

Correct the other team? That wasn't the half of it.

Literally hundreds of times in his life he walked out onto basketball courts—many times when he did not know any of the players on the court—and just took over. The basketball court was his domain. *Any* basketball court. He would just walk out and stop the game, demand the ball (and get it!) and then say what was on his mind.

"Boys, I'm sorry for interrupting your game, but I just had to talk to you. I've been sitting there watching you, and you seem like good boys. You seem to want to play this game. You like this game, don't you? And you want to be basketball players . . ."

He could see the difference immediately between kids just playing for fun (though he wondered how they could have fun doing what they did, fracking with the game) and kids who were trying to be real players. When he perceived that they were trying to be players (like kids who had obviously practiced dribbling a lot but dribbled too much in games, or kids who had devotedly practiced shooting but shot wildly), he felt compelled to help them. It was an obligation, not really a choice.

If you think that kids playing basketball down through the years were shocked to have their games interrupted by some intense, older stranger stopping them to offer instruction, you're right. But the story gets better!

Coach DV used to spend parts of every summer vacation on the beach at Lake Erie. Dozens of times, he would be sitting in the sand, enjoying the sun, and see a couple of kids come down to the beach carrying a football. Perhaps they would be wearing sleeveless football jerseys with numbers on them and he could see that they had lifted some weights. They were athletes—at least he assumed they were athletes—and he was ready to admire them.

He felt an affinity to athletes. Everywhere he went, he had the habit of meeting athletes and making connections. He often knew their coaches or someone they knew, or he had played against their father. The number of connections was incredible. He had a memory for such things and an appreciation for it. He knew the names of the guys on the other teams who had played softball or basketball against him, or his brothers, fifty years before. He cared about things like that, read the papers, loved sports and people—particularly sports people.

He could and did convey that sincere interest and appreciation to a couple of athletes instantaneously. He made them proud, via his interest and admiration, to be who they were. In many instances, he would meet an athlete somewhere and you could hear him say, "I know you. I saw your game last year against so-and-so; I remember that catch you made in the third quarter. It broke the game open."

If you have played sports, you know how much it means to be recognized for your efforts, to be remembered like that in a special, sincere way by a stranger. Then, should they find out that he was the Coach DV they had heard about, the appreciation he expressed became all the more meaningful.

A genuine friendship could arise out of a brief meeting like that. Those kinds of sports friendships were constants in Coach

DV's life. Hundreds, probably thousands of athletes have been touched in some way by Coach DV's heart-felt admiration. They remembered it and were buoyed by it.

In fact, it wasn't unusual for a star athlete to want to play his best game against Coach DV's team, not because he wanted to beat Coach DV, but because he wanted to impress him. Even stars on other teams thrived on Coach DV's admiration.

As low as Coach DV could make you feel when he was angry at you for crapping around, he could lift you proportionately by his appreciation. That kind of intensity, for expressing both anger and appreciation, is a very rare quality—a gift I think, though at times it seemed more like a curse.

When those two sleeveless-shirted football players started passing the ball back and forth, Coach DV couldn't help but watch. He'd put his book down and ignore a pageant of bikinis to watch two athletes catch football! No doubt he anticipated that he would eventually walk up to them, probably tell them, as he did so often, that they looked like fine young men. He'd ask them who they played for, when their season began, who their coach was, what positions they played.

Always he asked and listened with great interest and, even if they had never heard of Coach DV, they would leave saying to each other, "Isn't he a great guy?" Plus, they truly felt better about themselves. No one ever wondered why he was asking so many questions. It never seemed like prying. He conveyed real interest; and people, particularly athletes, would pour out their life stories to him. If they discovered he was a coach, they would wish they could play for him. If he told them they might not feel that way if they really played for him ("I holler a lot!"), they would be sure that wouldn't matter.

"Wouldn't it be great to play for a coach who had that kind of appreciation for athletics? So what if he did raise hell?" That was their way of thinking.

But what if those two football players, rather than catching balls and running hard and diving for low ones, instead had a lackadaisical approach? What if they moved slowly or bent down reluctantly when the ball wasn't thrown directly to them? What if they missed balls and *walked* to get them?

Were they just a couple of not-very-athletic kids on a beach in the summer?

Not to Coach DV. They were like many inner city kids in the Nineties: underprivileged, undervalued, under-taught, under-supervised, under-guided. It wasn't enough for Coach DV to observe such things as natural phenomena and to sigh and shake his head and muse over what today's youth were coming to.

Coach DV's father had come to America from Italy, one of the many poor immigrants in search of the Promised Land, willing to work hard and make a better life for future generations. America was about reverence and respect, hard work and determination, overcoming poverty during The Depression, and being (as Coach DV was) the first in a family to go to college. Coach DV had joined the United States Navy and left college during World War II. Like millions of others, he sailed through the Pacific and stopped at places like Pearl Harbor, Iwo Jima, and Midway.

These weren't just names to him. It was war, history, and life itself. Everyone had to do his part. You didn't sit back and complain. You did what you could. You owed effort to your country, to the task at hand, and to yourself. An obvious lack of effort, even by unknown teenagers throwing a football on a beach, irked Coach DV.

"Boys," he growled, suddenly able to stand it no longer, walking with his determined, pissed-off stride and announcing in his gruff, scare-the-shit-out-of-you voice: "I can't watch this any longer. If you aren't going to catch the ball and *run* after it, get out of my sight. *You are marring my vacation!*"

The two kids probably never had the opportunity to play under a tough, demanding coach. No doubt Coach DV did indeed scare the shit out of them.

That voice, that anger—everything about that intense, competitive demeanor—left *zero space* for smirks and for questions like, "Who the hell do you think you are, telling us how to catch football? We can do anything we want. It's a free country."

Non-athletes or noncompetitive people had no way of preparing to meet the fury that was Coach DV when suddenly angered.

(Athletes and competitive people didn't fare much better!)

The two would-be athletes slunk off, out of Coach DV's sight, where they couldn't mar his vacation any longer!

Imagine their conversations, once out of earshot. "What was with him? Was he some kind of nut? What was he talking about? What did *we* do? It's not like we kicked sand on his blanket or anything. We never got within twenty yards of him!"

They were right. They hadn't, and they wouldn't.

And they would never understand what they had missed. They would never know how Coach DV had given them the benefit of the doubt, how he had assumed they were high school football players, and how he would create such positive feelings in the same way his father must have envisioned what America could be like when he decided to leave everything and take a life-and-death risk by traveling, without money, across the ocean in 1902.

Kids playing sports lackadaisically, whether on a beach or on an opposing team, needed to be corrected, not because Coach DV wanted to scold them or show off how much he knew, but because they were Americans, because they all shared this great country and the wonderful opportunities that could come about through sports, and because no one had acquainted these kids with how special those sports experiences could be. Someone *had* to tell them; otherwise, a responsibility was being shirked.

Coach DV thought kids needed to be told that you don't put gum under a seat, toss candy wrappers on a beach, make noise in a library, or show disrespect to adults. You don't walk after a ball either, and you don't make lackadaisical efforts in sports. These things were anathema to Coach DV. "It just ain't right!" Coach DV wouldn't stand for it. Someone *had* to tell 'em, and Coach DV would—every time.

22.
AUXILIARY PLAYERS:
CHANGING WITH THE TIMES?

Rochester boys' basketball coach Bob Rauch played against De Venzio's offense as a guard for Wilkinsburg High School twenty-six years ago. Saturday night, as coach, Rauch got to view the veteran's offensive scheme yet another time. But once again, the result was not to his liking. Springdale won, 60-49 . . .

"DeVenzio uses the exact same offense he used when I played," said Rauch, "and he still wins with it."/

— Nick Neupauer
Sports correspondent

There's a rule some place. It's written down. I'm sure it's written down. It must be written down.

Auxiliary Players: Changing with the Times?

Late in his career, after the death of his wife (my mother) of thirty-three years, Coach DV made a major change. He left Western Pennsylvania, where he had grown up and coached all but one year of his life, and went to a small, affluent private school in Charlotte, North Carolina. Many people advised him not to go. "Southerners are different," they said. "Parents are too involved at a private school." Plus, the rival schools were older, wealthier, and bigger.

But Coach DV went anyway. And he won—in his very first year. For the first time in the school's history, they beat their biggest competition. For four straight years, they beat both big rivals each time they played. They won four straight conference championships and picked up a state title along the way.

Coach DV had successfully transported his style and approach to winning basketball and totally transformed the environment. He taught another group of basketball players how to win, and he altered the mentality at the school permanently.

But even more noteworthy about this phase of his life, he demonstrated the flexibility to adapt himself, although (many would say) rigidity had always been the key to his success. After all, Coach DV had long required that *his* way, the *only* way, the *one* way to win, was adhered to strictly.

One year in Charlotte, however, he had a player who fit the stereotypical private school mentality, which varied greatly from the demands that Coach DV considered essential during thirty successful years of coaching.

What is the private school mentality? It's never correct to generalize broadly, but to offer a sense of it: the family goes on vacation—skiing in Europe!—every Christmas, so the kid will miss two weeks of midseason practice, including the holiday basketball tournament. The kid has piano lessons on Thursday evenings, so he needs to leave practice early that day. The kid goes to dentists and doctors with specialties Coach DV can't pronounce. The family has an annual reunion, the kid has an opportunity to attend a prestigious leadership conference or to participate in a science fair, or he has a special test to take for a scholarship.

In brief, private school kids get all sorts of opportunities that public school kids don't. More opportunities—*distractions?*—were presented to some of his players in a single year at this private school than had ever happened in Coach DV's thirty years combined at public schools.

If you cut a kid for missing a practice at a private school (for having a test to take or for going on a family vacation), you might have to cut the whole team!

So how does a coach transform this kind of environment when it is constantly trying to transform him?

It's normally a struggle. For Coach DV, it was really quite simple, though.

"Boys, I know you have a lot of opportunities here, and I'd be the last one to try to prevent you from having those opportunities. But you have to make a decision. If you take all of these opportunities, you can't expect to be a winner. Winners have to make sacrifices. Winners have to make commitments. Winners have to say that they will make extraordinary efforts to honor those commitments.

"If *you* miss today's practice with a very acceptable excuse, and then *he* misses tomorrow's, and then Joe-Joe-Bean over there misses the next day's, you may all have very acceptable, very fine excuses, but you will also have a losing team that just doesn't practice enough together to become something special. You have to decide, boys, whether you are willing to pay the price. You have to decide what's important to you—and your parents have to decide—and you may have to cut out some family gatherings or some science fairs. I'm not saying you *should* do that; I'm just saying you *have* to do that if you want to win. Boys, I want to win, and I want to work with boys who want to win.

"If you don't want to do that, that's fine. We can stay good friends and I'll come to your piano recitals and I'll cheer for you if that's what you do at recitals, and I'll be happy to go see your exhibit at the science fair. I like those things; I have nothing against them. In fact, I honestly think a lot of you *should* put your time into those things instead of basketball. I'm just saying that if you want to be a basketball player, then you have to be a basketball player, and you can't do all of those other things."

Actually, Coach DV was more flexible on these sorts of things than many other dictatorial coaches. Frequently, he sincerely felt a kid should take a special opportunity. It just shouldn't happen very often, and it should definitely *not* happen when the opportunity in question was "a nice thing."

Sure, it would be "nice" to attend a leadership conference and to meet some kids from other schools and hear some speakers, but there was a thing called keeping a commitment ("stick-to-it-iveness"), which was even more important, according to Coach DV.

Coach DV didn't doubt that a leadership conference would be worthwhile; it merely wasn't sufficient reason for a kid to miss basketball practice. Private school kids had to make decisions. They had to be willing to miss a lot of "nice activities."

"If you are making an effort to do everything in your power to add to this team, then if you get some very special opportunity and need to miss a practice, sure you can go. But you can't approach this team as just another 'learning experience' alongside a whole list of nice activities. If *that* is your intention, then your basketball learning experience has to be intramural or YMCA, not on *my* team. Because basketball is my life, boys; it's my heart and soul."

Typically, as he did everywhere he coached, DV found a small core of kids willing to meet his demands; they enjoyed the success he promised. "Two or three kids out of each class, that's all you need," Coach DV used to say. "You don't need a lot of kids. You just need to find two or three each year willing to make that commitment, and you can be successful."

So Coach DV found his two or three from each class, even at this private school, and his teams won. But somehow, somewhere along the line, an anomaly "snuck" in.

First, the headmaster made a special request for a player. Then his parents called. Then a doctor said, "Being on the basketball team would be a healing experience for him . . . If there is any way . . ."

As inflexible as Coach DV may seem in some ways, he could be incredibly open-minded in others. "Sure, if it is truly this important, of course the kid can be on the team. We'll be happy to have him."

Actually, Coach DV had originally advised against it. He didn't believe it really could be that important. His experience taught him that players not fully committed ended up having negative experiences. All the hollering and intensity wasn't going to be tolerable for kids not fully committed. It wouldn't be important enough to them to do things right, to strive for perfection, to sacrifice and to suffer a little when necessary.

So, although he advised against it, he took the kid. By all standards of past experience, the kid should have driven The Coach crazy. The kid was the epitome of the private school mentality—every demanding coach's nightmare.

After begging for special consideration and a place on the team, the kids' parents did indeed inform Coach DV that the kid would not be able to attend the holiday practices and the tournament. *Family vacation!* After promising to alter his schedule to see the kid "at times not in conflict with the basketball team's schedule," the player's doctor scheduled appointments after school when the team had practice. The kid broke more rules and missed more practices in one month than all the players on all Coach DV's past teams put together. Yet Coach DV let him remain on the team.

When about to begin a meeting with his team, before taking the court for practice, Coach DV would look up from his notes and typically say something like, "Is everyone here?"

For thirty years, everyone was always there. Some were sick, wrapped in blankets, propped up with casts, or holding ice to some swelling part of their bodies, but they were there. They were always there.

Athletes discovered quickly how much that meant to Coach DV. "If you really want to play, you'll be here." If you chose to use an excuse, you might get away with it at the time. You would not be thrown off the team for one legitimate excuse, but that absence would often find its way into future comments and criticisms: "You see, boys, that's why you need to be here. When you aren't, these negative things happen, and we have no way to control them because you aren't here." As you can guess, his comments could get a lot more pointed than that.

It was simply easier to be there. Let Coach take a look at you and send you home. Then, there was no problem. But don't just stay home on your own. Don't dare let there be some doubt about your commitment; it wouldn't go that well for you after that. Better to demonstrate your commitment. Let Coach say, "What the hell are you doing here? You need to get home and get some sleep. Come back when you're healthy." That way, you would never hear about it again.

What was crucial to Coach DV was the desire. If you had desire, you would demonstrate it in a thousand ways, and there would be no doubt. He would love you—and send you home or get you to a hospital or drive you to a science fair and bring the whole team along! If you were working with him, he would work with you. But if you were working against him, it would be much better for everyone if there were no relationship at all.

So how was it that Coach DV would look up at least once per week and ask if everyone was there and find that One Private School Kid wasn't? Didn't it drive Coach DV crazy? Probably every player who ever played for him would have bet Coach DV would either quit or cut the kid or one day bring the kid's plattered head to practice.

But Coach DV chose none of the above. He kept the kid and labeled him "an auxiliary player," and he turned the whole issue into a point of humor instead of letting it bother him.

When you recall that often it seemed as though every tiny thing bothered Coach DV, that every noise, every comment, every different philosophy, and every parent was basically an unwelcome distraction for Coach DV, it is nearly impossible to conceive that he could have allowed this one kid the latitude that he did.

Was there a double standard?

"Double standard?" Coach DV said. "Hell no, there was a triple-triple, quadrupled, quintupled standard. And you can multiply *that* . . . But," Coach DV would add, "they tell me it's for a good reason."

Supposedly a grand team effort was keeping this kid alive, helping him to heal. Parents, teachers, administrators, headmaster, sixteen doctors and coaches were all in it together. Of course, Coach DV thought it was ridiculous. He totally disagreed with their idea that it "would mean a lot if the young man could play on the basketball team."

"Bullshit!" would have been Coach DV's typical reply. Bullshit was precisely how he viewed it. All of his instincts and past experience told him that a kid does not have a worthwhile experience when he is not fully committed to it. In fact, he probably even thought the experience was negative. But Coach DV had acquiesced to the experience and to the professional opinions of others—not out of weakness and not because he felt pressured.

He had always been willing to tell anyone that they could take a job and shove it if retaining the job required that he compromise his principles. But with The Kid, he didn't compromise his principles. He laughed at the situation. He had never had an auxiliary player in all of his years of coaching; perhaps it was time!

He explained it to his team. "Boys, people told me it would be different down here, and they were wrong. You guys have proved them wrong. You work hard; you're athletes and I'm proud of you. Keep it up. We can't rest on our laurels. We have to keep working if we plan to win the rest. You're going after it, and I really think you can do it if you're willing to keep working like you have been.

"Now, as for our auxiliary player, does anyone know where he is today? No? Well, okay, I appreciate your attitude on this. I've never had an auxiliary player before, and I'm not always sure what to do with one. But since he's not here too often, I guess I don't really have to think about it much, do I?" He laughed. It was so out of character and past experience for him to have a situation like this. "Just do me one favor, boys. Don't come up with any surprises. Don't suddenly miss a practice and have your parents call the school saying you have to be allowed on the team because I let The Kid stay on the team and he misses all the time.

"Your parents would be right, you would be right. But I think all of you know that we can only have one auxiliary player. This is the only one I've had in my career. I can only *have* one in my career. Tell your parents that, boys. There's a rule some place. It's written down. I'm sure it's written down. It must be written down." He finally said to his smiling captain, "Will you write it down somewhere?"

"Sure Coach, I'll write it down."

"You see, boys, it's written down somewhere. Or at least it's gonna be written down. So it's a rule. A coach can only have one auxiliary player in his career. Isn't life great? I thought I was going to get through my whole career without having one of those. But I got mine!

"Okay, that's enough of that. But I do appreciate your attitude, boys. We're gonna keep our auxiliary player because he has some problems and some people think that being on our team may help him." Coach DV laughed and shook his head. "You know I think that's a bunch of horse crap, but we won't talk about that anymore. Let's make sure we work hard and get a big win this weekend. Take five laps."

Coach DV simply redefined the distraction, allowed it to be humorous, gave the situation a name, and essentially dealt around it. He would stick the kid in practice situations whenever it was possible and convenient. Other than saying "Where's the auxiliary player?" he never made fun of the kid or made special mention. He let the kid be as much a part of the team as was possible under the circumstances. He didn't holler and scream at the kid, as he had *every* player who had played for him for thirty years or as he continued to do with *every* kid for the next ten years. But he let the kid wear a uniform, come to practice and participate, and he even put him in games at the end when the outcome was clearly decided.

He managed to remain fully himself in every way while divorcing himself from a situation he considered absurd. He couldn't possibly imagine how the experience could have helped the kid. He never thought it did. But he decided not to argue with the doctors, and he let them have their way.

He was the only auxiliary player Coach DV ever had in his career. There must truly be an exception to every rule! It's written down somewhere.

23.
FILMS, NEWSPAPERS, AND CHAMPIONS

He gave me a certain foundation of energy. I mean, as a result of having had the experience of playing under Coach, I have a certain capacity to withstand adversity that I otherwise wouldn't have. Because, when I start to feel sorry for myself, I always think of Coach DV in the background, standing over my shoulder, yelling like he always did in practice: 'Goddammit Hepler, you lazy ass!' "

— Robert Hepler
Former Coach DV player

WHAT HAPPENED? DID YOU DO ANYTHING? I DIDN'T DO ANYTHING.

Films, Newspapers, and Champions

It was Coach DV's last year of coaching—his last team—and predictably, they had won their conference, breezing past everyone, undefeated. Coach DV enjoyed coaching this group. They worked hard. They were gentlemen, and they were over-achieving. They were ranked at or near the top of the polls for Western Pennsylvania basketball. And why shouldn't they be? They kept beating people.

Coach DV had that aura. He had won the Western Pennsylvania championship two years earlier, and now he was back again. But was he mellowing, finally? After forty years of coaching, that Southern private school experience was behind him.

Mellowing?

His team was preparing for the playoffs. Coach DV had gotten a videotape of the first-round opponent. If his team lost, that other team would be his last round opponent, since playoffs were single elimination. One loss and Coach DV would call it a career.

The team was assembled in a classroom. All but one player was there. He wasn't late, though; it was still fifteen minutes before practice was scheduled to start.

In the front of the room, Coach DV was looking over some notes and checking the VCR to make sure the tape was ready to play. He had already been assured several times—and shown by his assistant—that all he had to do was press the "on" button, and the tape would play. Still, he was always skeptical of technology. He didn't understand machines very well. He still hadn't learned to tape a program on his own VCR, which he had gotten as a gift. Actually, he could do it in an emergency, but he would rather not. It would mean he would have to read the owner's manual, and he didn't like reading owners' manuals.

But in this case, everything was prepared. The tape was in

the slot, the TV was already on. Coach DV knew where the VCR's "on" button was, so he was ready. He looked at his watch just as the last player walked through the door. Everyone was present. There were still thirteen minutes till the scheduled practice time, so even the last player to arrive was thirteen minutes early. That was good. Almost like "Lombardi time." When the feared and respected Green Bay Packer football coach called a meeting for 3:00, you were late if you weren't there by 2:30!

Coach DV wasn't as strict as Lombardi, but he admired Vince Lombardi and was every bit as punctual himself, always at least an hour early for anything he did. He expected his players to arrive early for everything too. But thirteen minutes ahead of schedule wasn't bad for the whole team. He had been waiting for that last player, but he wasn't fidgeting. Thirteen minutes was okay.

He looked up from his notes for a moment. The whole team was seated. Then he checked the VCR one more time. It was ready. He was about to turn it on, to go over this first opponent in the playoffs that he definitely did not want to be the last. He looked up.

Then he suddenly blew up. "Get out! Everyone get out! Get up, get the hell out of here and go home. You guys don't want to win a championship. Get out of here. Move! Get out! Go home! If you want to win, come back tomorrow. I'm tired of this crap! You decide if you want to win. Practice is over. Go home! That's all for today."

The team scurried out of the room. No one said a word. They knew better. It was never difficult to know whether or not Coach DV was serious, and no one had a shred of doubt now. Coach DV was super pissed.

Coach DV shook his head in disgust, and he mumbled.

Outside, as soon as the players were certain they were beyond Coach DV's hearing, in a part of the school where Coach DV wouldn't go, they turned to each other.

"What happened? . . . Did you do anything? . . . I didn't do anything . . . I was just sitting there waiting for Coach to turn on the tape . . . He wasn't even mad . . . No one said a word . . . the place was completely quiet . . . Did *you* do anything? I didn't do anything . . . What is Coach so pissed about? . . . Damn, he was hot! . . . He's mad at *some*one. Did *you* do anything?"

No one had done anything.

Was Coach DV going crazy? Had the pressure of forty years of coaching finally gotten to him? People always said he was going to have a heart attack some day, the way he carried on and got so emotional. Had he finally gone off the deep end? Did he really blow up for nothing?

Actually, none of the players suspected that Coach DV had blown up for nothing. Sure, he got plenty angry. He blew up over all sorts of things. But for nothing? It wasn't his style. Right or wrong, he was never short of reasons. He was usually quick to say exactly what was bothering him. "You can't play basketball like *that*!"

But this time was different. Coach hadn't said one word except that they didn't want to win; go home, get out.

One player knew he was guilty. The Captain. He knew by Coach DV's stare. But he didn't really feel guilty. All he had been doing was quietly reading the newspaper. He didn't say much as his teammates discussed the situation. He himself didn't know what Coach DV was mad about.

At home, when the players told their parents what had happened, there were mixed reactions. "He's a loser! . . . He's crazy! . . . I never did understand that man . . . He's gonna have a heart attack some day . . . I think the pressure is finally getting to him; he's been coaching a long time."

But there were other views, too. "I doubt if he blew up over nothing. Were you paying attention? I played for him myself, remember, and I never knew him to get mad over nothing. Someone did something, I'll guarantee that."

The opinions were quite divergent at that time and no less mixed the next day after the team came back, found out what had happened, practiced, and prepared for the playoffs.

Coach DV had thrown the entire team out of practice and lost a valuable preparation day going into the playoffs, all because one kid was quietly reading the paper when Coach DV was ready to turn on the tape. There was nothing else. That was it.

How could such a tiny thing warrant so dramatic a response? The kid was Captain. He was a senior. He had had a very fine year, perhaps the team's Most Valuable Player, and was certainly one of the top three players on the team. Certainly the team's most consistent performer. He was a fine student. A future good citizen. He was reading the paper, curious about the world, and maximizing his time while waiting for the last player to show up. What could possibly be wrong with that? What should he do, sit there with his hands folded while waiting for the last player? Or make small talk? What difference did it make where he read the paper? The last kid, the kid who arrived thirteen minutes early could have been out in the hall reading the paper all that time. Coach couldn't be angry at him!

What was so bad about reading the paper?

Coach DV loves newspapers. In fact, a History teacher for over thirty years, he was a nut for current events. There were current event questions on every one of his tests. He marveled throughout his life that it was possible to buy a paper—with all that information in it every day—for just a dime. It was the one commodity whose rising prices through the years didn't cause him to lament. He loved newspapers, and he liked the kind of kid who would read newspapers. Everything about his History classes was an attempt to get students interested and curious about the world around them. So how could he, of all people, blow up over one fine young man quietly reading the paper before practice was even scheduled to start?

It was clear in the mind of Coach DV.

He just wasn't that good at articulating his feelings, at least not when he was angry. But had he told his players his feelings at the time, they would have been very much like this:

"Winning a championship, boys, is a very special thing. I've been playing ball and coaching my entire life, and I've only had a couple of them where you go all the way and win your last game of the season. These aren't just games. And if you don't understand that—I can't expect you to understand, you're young—I have to try to help you to understand. I have to push you and prod you, because someday you'll thank me for it.

"It wasn't reading the newspaper that bothered me, boys, I hope you know that by now. It was the fact that we are a team, and we were all there, waiting . . .

"One loss and we're out. We're finished. Our season is over and we pack up our uniforms. It's that simple. Most of the games are going to be decided by a few points. And if we do that little bit extra, if we get those few extra points, then we are the winners, and *we* come back again.

"Then the papers write about us. Reporters ask us questions. People want to look at us walking into arenas. People come from all over to watch us play. You guys know what a good feeling that is. Most of you were with us two years ago. You remember what a great feeling that was. It was great, boys, it was really something special.

"Don't you want that for yourself? Don't you realize what a slim, tiny, minuscule difference there is between winning and losing? Don't you realize what 'single elimination' means? Most teams across the country aren't even playing now. They didn't win their conferences, so they aren't playing anymore. Only the conference winners now, boys, and we're one of those. We have this one chance.

"Do you think the other playoff teams are just taking the days off? Do you think they aren't staying up at night thinking about how to beat us? Do you think they won't be willing to dive on the floor or run into a wall or crack you with an elbow to the nose if that can help them beat us?

"Other people want to win, too, boys; you don't win just by going through the motions. I thought you knew that by now. I guess I threw you all out of practice yesterday because I was mad at myself, that I hadn't gotten through to you after all this time.

"Was it just Brian reading the paper? Of course not. I think he's been our most consistent player. I've been so pleased with the year you've had, Brian, and with the relationship we've had. And the point is, I guess I was thinking, while just waiting to turn on the machine, that we aren't the kind of team that deserves to win a championship. A championship team would have been crowded around the table *before* I turned the machine on, asking what to look for, asking who their men would be, asking if I thought we could beat them, asking how big they are, asking, asking, asking, asking.

"While we waited all that time for the last player to arrive, not one player asked a question. Not one player was curious enough to be seeking an edge. Not one of you, even though you've been around me for three years, thought to ask a question. Not one of you was impatient to know about the other team. No one did *anything*. No one stepped up and acted like a champion. No one stood up and said, 'I did extra things.' Did you do extra things?

"It wasn't the newspaper itself, boys. I heard someone say Brian was just 'maximizing' his time. But that's not it, I hope you understand. My own son, the one who's an advertising executive, he even said it—and I'll have to admit, I never even knew he was such a winner. But he said his boss in Warren, Ohio, used to say: 'I don't want an employee maximizing *his* time. I want an employee maximizing *my* time.'

"I think you know, boys, that I think education is important. I've always said that. I don't think basketball is the most important thing in the world. Not at all. But I've also said over and over again, if you're gonna play this game, you gotta play it. You gotta give it your heart and soul.

Should Coach DV have thrown the team out of practice? Should the Captain have been reading the paper? You decide.

And you can also decide how much it hurt the team to take that day off versus how much it may have helped them to have the confrontation, to wake up, to have to reexamine their commitment to give it everything they had. You never know such things for sure. Or do you?

Coach DV's team won that next game easily, and another and another. They didn't win the state championship, though. They lost to the team that did win it—by one point.

24.
THE EXHILARATION OF APPROVAL

The bottom line is what these young men learned and took from the experience. They may realize some now, but only later will they really understand how important the lessons you taught are. Thanks for giving so much to our young people.

— Dr. Ronald J. Wasilak
School district superintendent

NO ONE ELSE HAD EVER COMPLIMENTED THEM SO FORCEFULLY, SO MEANINGFULLY, SO PENETRATINGLY.

The Exhilaration of Approval

It would be unfair to Coach DV to end this book without paying homage to his ultimate achievement. After forty years of coaching, through all of the tough, demanding, and sometimes torturous times, nearly every player he ever coached respected and liked him.

A special "Coach DV Night" roast, attended by nearly 300 friends and former players from as far away as California attested to the esteem in which so many held him.

Among the many reasons (the toughness, the consistency, the honesty) that have caused four decades of athletes to appreciate him, none is more compelling than his ability to praise.

Much of that quality must be considered in context. Realizing that Coach DV was dissatisfied and angry most of the time, it was a tremendous relief and a real joy to suddenly find yourself, if only momentarily, basking in Coach DV's approval for a play or a pass or a steal performed exactly as Coach DV wanted to see it.

Secondly, as you can imagine, anyone so able to reach people so penetratingly in critical or negative ways usually has the proportionate ability to reach them in complimentary and positive ways.

When Coach DV erupted with praise—"Now *that's bas*ketball!"—you couldn't help but feel ten or eleven or fifteen feet tall.

As demanding as Coach DV was, he wasn't stingy with praise. If you gave him what he wanted, his joy, his gratitude, his reaction was as spontaneous and effulgent as any of his angry outbursts.

Coach DV simply hated bad basketball and loved good basketball. What a joy it was to get to the point in your career where you could relax him on the bench (somewhat!) and then bring him to his feet again and again, hearing those spontaneous "Yeahs!" that would literally erupt. Help on defense, be alert, hit the open man, *move!* When you did those things, the benefits were glorious.

"*That* is *bas*ketball . . . *That's* what I'm talking about, boys, did you see that? Watch that. Watch him. *That's* the way you play this game."

Most of the players who ever played for Coach DV would probably admit that no one else had ever been so often disgusted with them and so intensely critical of them. But nearly all would also say that no one else had ever complimented them so forcefully, so meaningfully, so penetratingly.

When Coach DV complimented you, you never forgot it. You had finally arrived. Your whole life seemed validated.

When a not-particularly-good player happened to make an uncharacteristically good play, Coach DV would often fumble for his whistle and then blow it and blow it. Five, ten, maybe twenty seconds, he would blow that whistle. The whole team would laugh. They knew Coach DV would never take that much time to hold in his anger. If he was blowing that whistle and rolling his fist in the air, the team knew the unexpected pleasant surprise had happened.

Was it demeaning? Was he making fun of a kid who so seldom did anything meriting praise? Not at all. No one got much praise anyway in Coach DV's particularly demanding practice environment; but when you got it, it was *real*, and that extended whistling wasn't one bit mockery.

"Call out the fire department!" Coach DV would yell. "Bigsy got a rebound!" But he wasn't belittling the kid.

"Now you see, Bigsy. You can do it. You *can* get the ball. You have the ability. You looked tough that time. You really did. If you play like that, no one's gonna beat us. Wasn't that fun? I mean it, all kidding aside, didn't you enjoy getting that ball and feeling taller and tougher than everyone else? Wasn't it a good feeling *tearing* that ball out of there? You looked great that time, Bigs, really you did. I felt tough that time just watching you! You *looked* like a *bas*ketball player."

If Bigsy could grab a few rebounds like that in a game, he

might come back to the bench for a timeout or quarter break and get a hard slam to the chest that he would never forget. It would feel better than a two hour massage!

"That's the way to *grab* that ball, Bigsy. Now you're playing like a *bas*ketball player."

The admiration and gut-level intensity of positive feeling in those few words defined the meaning of the word inspiration. A kid who felt long abused but who had finally "gotten the idea" would experience a depth of joy that few other endeavors would ever afford him; and he would be pushed to greater heights of achievement and self-pride than he ever thought possible. Coach DV could make a kid feel miserable, but he could also lift him to great heights.

There simply aren't many feelings equal to the exhilaration of basking in the radiance of Coach DV's approval. It sure wasn't easy to get to that point, or to stay there. But if you did . . .

Coach DV. Now *that's* a *bas*ketball coach.

Coach DV
Unrelenting perfectionist

Referees beware. Though usually more concerned with the performance of his team than of the referees, officials ofter experienced his emotions at close reange. Here, however, he is praising a good play.

He depised premature celebration and never considered a game over until the last echo of the final buzzer had faded. In this photo, the bench reacts excitedly over a victory while Coach DV still concentrates intently on the last second of action.

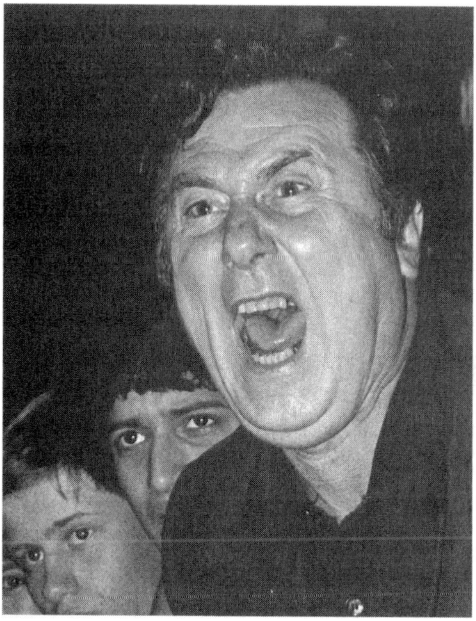

Unlikely as it may seem from his expression here, Coach DV has been admired by thousands of players, students, and fans.

Elated or angry? Sometimes you couldn't tell. In this instance, Coach DV was very happy with a player whose effort had helped pull out a close victory.

For 40 years, Coach DV forcefully and continually corrected mistakes, never being content with mediocrity whether his team was ahead or behind.

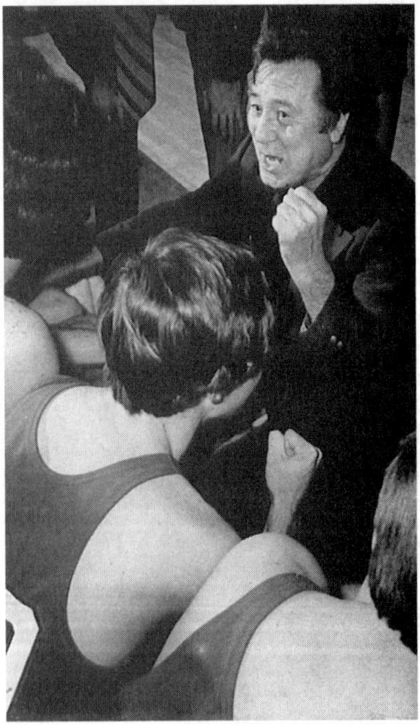

His use of time-outs frequently contradicted conventional wisdom, but he called every one of them with a definite purpose in mind and a clear view of what had to be done.

Coach DV and his son, Dick DeVenzio

"Play like a human being!"

Though always amiable prior to tip-off and generally friendly after a game, Coach DV was immersed emotionally in every play of the competition.

Appendix

People Talk about Coach DV

Coach DV had a profound impact on many people, and that impact continues. Following is a sampling of comments made through the years in letters, on television, at hall of fame award banquets, and at a special "roast" called Coach DV Night. The words included come from nationally-known coaches, other basketball and football coaches, school administrators, sportswriters, and former players and students.

Tony Smith, a sportswriter for the *Valley News Dispatch*, began a column on December 21, 1988, with these appropriate words (not knowing that perhaps Coach DV's finest season lay still ahead):

"The Coach. The Legend. The Motivator. Words of praise, admiration, and respect have been heaped on the shoulders of Chuck DeVenzio over the years..."

One of the finest tributes comes from Colonel Bob C. Anderson, whose work with terrorism and special operations for the Air Force put him in the middle of events during Desert Storm. He wasn't a star for Coach DV. In fact, he didn't even play during his senior year while he concentrated on music. However, he thought enough about the influence of Coach DV to write a long letter to him soon after he returned from Saudi Arabia. He made it very clear that Coach DV's influence had an impact on the things he did in the Middle East, even though he had played for DV in the early Sixties, thirty years earlier!

"I've recently returned from a little adventure called Desert Storm and waded through a stack of papers built up during my seven months in the desert. I read about your retirement and couldn't let it pass without sending you a letter of thanks. Your example has been very important to me over the years and helped to guide me in many tight situations.

You taught me to play basketball and I will be forever grateful... Watching a master coach and teacher at work shaped my early perception of excellence. I vividly remember what a rush it was to be standing in the lunch line in ninth grade, having you compliment me on my play in junior high, and then being told that you were looking forward to my move to high school. President Bush has recognized my work in terrorist situations and, while I'm grateful for that, your kind words that day had a greater impact since my self image was being formed.

When I got to tenth grade, I had a chance to watch you coach... to this day I am amazed how you seemed to sense how to get the most out of each of us. Some responded only when you punctuated your point with an airborne basketball, while others like myself responded when you explained what went wrong and offered an approach to correct the mistake... I first learned the need to differentiate in a leadership position by watching you operate. I think a great deal of my success in Saudi Arabia has to be rooted in watching you like a hawk during my brief basketball career at Springdale High School.

I wish my boys would have had a chance to play for you...

...I'm a consultant to U.S. Special Operations Command in psychological operations and terrorism... I was Chief of Mental Health in our desert hospital... doing this stuff is a lot like playing basketball for you: it ain't dull and you learn a lot about yourself.

You have touched the lives of so many of us and I, for one, will be eternally grateful... Out in Saudi we were fortunate to have a guy like Schwartzkoff calling the shots. You both have much in common... Thanks again for being one of the all time great coaches and people. You age like a fine wine and I can hardly wait to discover what your next project will be. You are a treasure!"

Dr. Warren Ferguson, who played for DV in the late Fifties and went on to Brown University, has remained a close personal friend of Coach DV. On Coach DV Night in 1980, Dr. Ferguson's comments brought tears to the eyes of most of the audience.

"In the past twenty-four years I've made no decision in my life, major or minor, that has not been directly influenced by the values, the attitudes and the morality of Coach DeVenzio.

A guy named Eric Burn wrote a book about the psychology of human destiny, and he contends that each person, under the powerful influence of individuals close to him, writes the script that will govern the general course of his life. And in my life, the individual that Eric Burn describes was Coach DeVenzio. Not because he was my coach, but because in the three years I spent at Springdale High School, he talked to me, he listened to me, he gave me his time, and most important of all he gave a damn; and the resulting impact on my life has been absolutely profound.

I have two kids at home and, like most people with kids, I worry about them all the time. Since they [were] born, I prayed for them each day, not for Olympic gold medals or NCAA titles or that they become medical doctors. I pray to god for just one thing: that someday, somewhere along the way into each of their lives will walk their own personal Coach DV. And the day god answers that prayer is the day I won't worry about my kids anymore."

John Hince, who played for Coach DV in the mid-Sixties and who became a coach himself, echoed Dr. Ferguson's feelings, as many have, by writing to Coach DV about how much he wished that DV could coach his sons. Hince wrote this letter in April of 1989.

"Congratulations on a tremendous year... You continue to inspire young men to do their best... I hope that in my seventeen years of coaching I inspired one young man as much as you have inspired a multitude of young men... I wish there was some way it could be arranged that you would one day coach my three sons."

Perhaps surprisingly, football coaches down through the years seemed to value Coach DV's style and methods even though his teaching didn't precisely apply to their sport. Below are the words of three football coaches, a major college coach who admired DV, a local high school coach who had never met him, and another high school coach who had starred on one of DV's basketball teams in addition to being a football player. The first brief comments come from Frank Cignetti, at the time the head football coach at the University of West Virginia.

"I have always had great admiration for you as a coach and feel you always do an outstanding job with your material."

These comments came from a letter written by Quaker Valley football coach, John Nusskern, of Sewickley, Pennsylvania.

"Allow me to add my congratulations to the many you have already received. Your basketball team was great this season... Much was made of your team's offensive ability, but your defense was something to behold... You seem to have a gift for the coaching profession. May you continue to contribute for many years to come."

Ray Carion, head coach of the Kirtland High School football team in Kirtland, Ohio, wrote these words in 1967. It is interesting to note that in 1967, twelve years after he played for Coach DV, he still felt it important to express the regret he felt for having let down Coach DV in 1955!

"I take a great deal of pride in telling others that I once played for DV. But I should like to offer my thanks from another

standpoint. It comes by way of intangibles that few others (other than coaches) realize. I feel that you, Coach, more than any other person, are responsible for me enjoying the type of life I now enjoy... I like to think that on the court we were about as close as a player and coach can be. I've played for a great many coaches but none was able to instill the fierce competitive spirit that you did. Maybe you didn't actually instill that in me, but believe me, Coach, you made me realize that it's the right and only way of going about things. If I'm ever fortunate enough to have some young man feel toward me as I have felt toward you, Coach, I'll have to say that what I am doing is right. You know, Coach, I've never told you this but I still feel that I let you down in February of 1955 when Tarentum beat us for the Section... I only wish it could have been Ray Carion starting on one of your state championship teams so that I could have repaid DV for playing such an important part in my life. Good luck and continued success, Coach. And thank you."

Coach DV kept up a continuous personal friendship and correspondence with some of the best known coaches in the history of basketball. Below are just three examples. The first is from Chuck Daly, who was the 1992 U.S. Olympic Coach, former head coach of the two-time NBA Champion Detroit Pistons, the New Jersey Nets, and the Orlando Magic. The telegram read:

"Congratulations on your many years of dedication and success... May next season gleam with another championship team. When you see the USA in your new Chevrolet, be sure to come see us."

Daly was referring to the new car Coach DV received from the town of Ambridge, Pennsylvania, for winning the State Championship in 1967. Coach DV had known Daly when he was a high school coach in Punxsutawney, Pennsylvania, and they spoke later at some clinics and banquets after Daly became an assistant at Duke University.

With University of North Carolina coach Dean Smith, Coach

DV maintained a personal friendship that lasted over twenty-five years. DV coached one of Smith's first team All-Americans, Dennis Wuycik. Coach Smith wrote the following brief words to be read at a banquet in DV's honor.

"Few coaches could have meant as much to a high school basketball player as Chuck DeVenzio has to so many."

John Wooden, considered by most basketball people as the greatest coach of all time, has exchanged many letters with Coach DV. Most are too personal in nature to be included here. Both Coach DV and Coach Wooden shared the tragedy of having their longtime, successful marriages end with the death of their wives. Both were nearly devastated by those deaths. Wooden wrote in August of 1985:

"We do have much in common and no one who has not experienced what we have would understand... Your kind words and continued concern are deeply appreciated."

Two school superintendents, one of whom played for Coach DV, offer a feeling for what administrators felt about him. In spite of the antics that could anger parents, most of the administrators with whom DV worked had a very high regard for him, both as a coach and as a teacher.

Dr. Ken Scholtz, Superintendent of the Hampton Township School District, played for DV in the Fifties and wrote many congratulatory messages to DV in the years following, including this one in 1989.

"Congratulations on your championship. You clearly out-coached your opponent and once again got 150 percent from your players (that's your greatest strength!!). I hope you fully realize the indelible impression you've made on so many of us. We love you for it. You're the best!"

Dr. Ronald Wasilak, Superintendent of the Allegheny Valley School District (which includes Springdale High School where

DV coached for more than twenty years), wrote these words to Coach DV.

"For the past few weeks I have been trying to collect my thoughts about the glorious season just completed. Not only did you and the team make history, you made many people take notice of Springdale... The only explanation for such success is the coaching and leadership that you gave to that team. You gave me and all of the fans thrills that we will never forget. In addition and obviously more importantly, you produced a degree of pride and unity in the school and community that is unprecedented in my twenty-seven years of recollection. I heartily thank you for that... The bottom line is what these young men learned and took from the experience. They may realize some now, but only later will they really understand how important the lessons you taught are. Thanks for giving so much to our young people."

Coach DV took great pride in his interest in students—not just star basketball players, but all of the students who attended the high schools where he taught. Many of his former students, including women who never played basketball, wrote letters to DV after one or another of his teams won championships. DV received hundreds of letters like these throughout his teaching and coaching career.

This first letter came from DeDe Felices in 1989.

"Even though I was a terrible student in your class, I look back and wonder what made you so special to me—and then I remembered—you always made me feel special. You always took the time to be tolerant of another "Baker" and you seemed to really care... I loved you then and I love you now. You did the same thing again this week. You're just a very special person, always encouraging others to feel special."

Nick Pinchok and his wife were students in DV's American History classes in the early Sixties. Nick, I think, played baseball for Coach DV.

"You must have many fond memories of your career as one of the most successful coaches in the history of Pennsylvania. Judy and I both have a warm spot in our hearts when we talk about you and your tremendous achievements in athletics. Our children have never met you, but they feel like they know you because of our Coach DV stories. We appreciate your friendship, your infectious laughter, and the pride you brought to Springdale as basketball and baseball coach. You are truly a very special, caring person that we will always remember with great affection."

Marcia Dechene was a History student of DV's in 1978. She wrote this letter near the end of that year.

"I have never written a letter like this before, but this is a must. You have to be one of the very best teachers I have ever had, and I am saying this truthfully. You showed so much enthusiasm for History and your classes. We need more teachers like you... you sure made class an interesting, fun, learning process. I wish every class was like that. Your sense of humor was unlike any other man's I have ever seen... I wish so much you would not retire. The school needs you... You probably think I'm writing this hoping to get a better grade, but the reason I'm writing is that I would start crying if I told it to your face. Love..."

Finally, DV has scrapbooks and boxes filled with letters from former players who made a point, often many years later, to write letters expressing how much their high school basketball careers meant to the course of their lives. This first is from Tom Butler, a player at North Allegheny High School with whom DV did not get along at all when Butler played for DV.

"From what I read in the paper, it sounds as though you have the makings of another very good team, and I know you will bust their collective asses to make sure they reach their full potential... Wins and losses aside Coach, I know for sure that your current group of players will take with them lessons far more important than learning when to switch responsibilities as the ball rotates in the matchup zone. As many of us did, your guys will learn that

no one person is more important than the team and that if you work together towards a common goal, all things are possible, but that you have to work hard because nothing in life is easy. I carry around these and other thoughts I learned from you and have applied them successfully... I hope you have another great year. Thank you for more than you realize."

Rich Gass, now a chief financial officer with a major company in Dallas, also played at North Allegheny High School for DV.

"I never thanked you for the things you taught me at North Allegheny. I didn't play basketball beyond high school. But, with your help, I was able to develop character traits that I have been able to apply in my life. I developed self-confidence playing under you. You motivated me to persevere under adversity. You taught me the importance of hard work. You also told me to have "gumption" and "not to take crap off anybody." I know these aren't eloquent words, but they are your words and they had a lot of meaning to a high school kid."

Ken Rankin, one of DV's players in the Fifties, wrote these lines in a college term paper.

"From DeVenzio I learned to look at basketball as something entirely different and more exciting than I had known before. He made a boy want to put out his best ability at all times.

His quick decisions and wise judgment gave us many close games in the closing minutes. A sixth sense told him when a man on the bench was ready to do the job a first stringer had failed on. He knew how to handle boys, and that in itself is a great asset to any coach. The rough voice came just when it was needed to drive us out of a lazy streak. The easy voice could talk us out of tightening up and being nervous with just as much meaning. DV believed that a boy with little ability, but with a heart to play, was worth more than a star with a wrong attitude.

DV ran us until my legs were fifty pounds heavier. Then he kept running us some more. Letting your man get ahead of you in this game is a deadly sin; if he does, the only way to stop him is to foul or do a rubber man act in blocking the shot. If I fouled him, I was hopeless, and if I blocked the shot, I was a bum for letting him loose in the first place.

When the game arrived we forgot about our gripes; we knew we were a prepared team. We were conditioned to play to the best of our ability."

The final words come from a letter from Hultz Page, one of Coach DV's close personal friends, who played on DV's team in 1948.

"I know if he wouldn't have coached in 1948, I probably wouldn't have played. I think I did what he asked of me, even though I wasn't a star player... He taught me discipline and desire. I love him for this. He's been a coach, a friend, a brother, and at one time in my life, a father. I love him for this."

Index

A
Afraid to shoot, 56, 97
Anderson, Bob, 96, 171

B
Balanced scoring, 1, 56
Beaver High School, 106
Bigsy, 53, 55, 61-66, 161-162
Birch, Paul, 121
Bird, Larry, 48, 50-51
Borneo, 55
Broken wide open, 30
Bruno, Larry, 108
Bush, George, 172
Butler, Tom, 28, 178

C
Caboose, 42
Carion, Ray, 17, 174-175
Carson, Curt, 15-16, 102
Catholic, 69-70
Chinese, 20
Choo, Foo Man, 88
Churovia, Bob, 67
Cignetti, Frank, 174
Clowe's, Barney, 94
Complicated things, 132
Conley, Jim, 52
Cutoff at the pass, 42

D
Daly, Chuck, 175
Dartmouth University, 68
Dechene, Marcia, 178
Depasquale, Phil, 54
Derlink, Jack, 56, 86
DeVenzio, Dave, 9, 110-112
DeVenzio, Huck, 9, 58

E
Eggs in tail, 42
Einstein, Albert, 19
Estridge, Billy, 22

F
Felices, Dede, 177
Ferguson, Denny, 47, 55-56, 173
Ferguson, Warren, 47, 173

G
Galcik, John, 59
Gass, Rich, 82, 179
Going near lines, 59
Gold, 20-carat, 30
Good Lord, the, 71, 96-97,

103-104
Gowing, Dale, 3
Great Depression, the, 40, 141

H

Harvard University, 68
Heimbuecher, Jack, 61
Heininger, Jason, 37
Hepler, Robert, 68-69, 152
Hince, John, 113, 173
H-O-R-S-E, 54

I

Illness, because of, 70
Interrupting games, 138

J

Joe Joe Bean, 29, 33, 42, 145
Jordan, Michael, 49

K

Klausing, Chuck, 108
Kruth, Jerry, 48

L

Lake Erie, 139
Little League Baseball, 134
Little Sisters of the Poor, 117
Lombardi, Vince, 154
Loving mistakes, 127

M

Mistakes, willing to make, 64
Mr. Equilibrium, 100
Murphy's Law, 59

N

Namath, Joe, 108
Nelson, Vernon, 22, 100-101
Neupauer, Nick, 143
Never give anything, 106, 110
New Castle, 42
No lead is big enough, 106, 112
Nusskern, John, 174

O

Once per career, 8
Onufer, Mike, 35
Ostrowski, Walt, 11, 54
Osvick, Rick, 41

P

Packer, Billy, 2
Page, Hultz, 180
Pearl Harbor, 141
Petruny, Joe, 55, 64-65
Pittsburgh Press, 72
Pinchok, Nick & Judy, 91, 177
Play nice, 75
Preferential treatment, 54
Private school mentality, 144, 147
Providence Day School, 105, 144
Purgatory, 70

R

Rankin, Ken, 133, 179
Rauch, Bob, 143
Ready to move, 20
Riley, Tom, 79
Robertson, Oscar, 37
Robinson, Wes, 105
Robak, John J., 137

S

Scholtz, Dr. Ken, 176
Score!, 102
Shutout, 112
Slencak, Brian, 157-158

Smith, Dean, 31, 104, 122-123, 125, 175
Smith, Tony, 171
Snake-terror noise, 61, 66
Spacing, 130-132
Stick-to-itive-ness, 146
Susa, Larry, 53

T

Trotting, 18
Turley, 43-45

V

Van Winkle, Rip, 68-69
Vigrass, Tim, 53

W

Warren, Ohio, 158
Wasilak, Dr. Ronald, 159, 176
West Virginia, 93
Wooden, John, 104, 176
World Coaches Federation, 132
Wuycik, Dennis, 97-99, 176

Z

Zurisko, Damien, 69

ABOUT THE AUTHOR

Dick DeVenzio gave his life to sports and to a set of beliefs, ideas and convictions mostly related to the intelligent pursuit of excellence in sports. The son of a very successful basketball coach, Dick grew up wanting to be a basketball star. That led to daily schedules and all-day practicing by the time he was in 7th grade. By 10th grade, he was a varsity starter, averaging 20 points a game—at 5′-6″, and the next year he averaged 30—at 5′-9″. In his senior year, he led Ambridge High School to an undefeated state championship, and his team is still considered the best ever to play in Pennsylvania. His name is in the Basketball Hall of Fame, on Parade Magazine's 1967 All-American First Five.

Two years later, at Duke University, Dick was an All-ACC selection, and in 1971, a First Team Academic All-American.

After graduating from Duke, Dick played and coached professional basketball in Europe and South America and founded the now nationally acclaimed Point Guard College.

Considered by many to be a basketball genius and a gifted writer, Dick's writings and basketball programs have inspired and influenced countless coaches and athletes. He died in 2001 at age 52.

OTHER BASKETBALL BOOKS BY PGC FOUNDER

STUFF: Good Players Should Know

Stuff Good Players Should Know may very well be the best book ever written for basketball players. It is conversational and easy to understand, yet filled with subtle insights into the game of basketball. STUFF is page after page of creative concepts, common sense, and special tips that cannot be found anywhere else. STUFF is like having a coach right beside you, in your room, discussing the fine points of the game. Basketball fans will enjoy it, but players won't do without it.

RUNNIN' THE SHOW

Runnin' The Show spells out what it takes to be a real leader on a basketball court. How can a coach get the most out of his players? How can a player make everyone around her better and do the little things that lead to championship performance? Leaders have to sell their dreams, get players to work together, inspire teamwork, and understand people, attitudes and motivation. This is the last book Dick DeVenzio ever published and is a treasure for leaders in all walks of life.

THINK LIKE A CHAMPION

Think Like A Champion is a guide to championship performance for student-athletes. A treasury of practical advice broken down into 122 short sections on situations that athletes must face. Covers everything from choking under pressure, lack of confidence and playing with teammates you don't like, to shooting slumps, academics and how to increase your speed and agility.